FEDERAL THEATRE PLAYS

A Da Capo Press Reprint Series

FRANKLIN D. ROOSEVELT
AND THE ERA OF THE NEW DEAL

GENERAL EDITOR: FRANK FREIDEL

Harvard University

FEDERAL THEATRE PLAYS

Edited for the Federal Theatre
by Pierre De Rohan

Federal Theatre project

Introduction by Hallie Flanagan

DA CAPO PRESS · NEW YORK · 1973

Library of Congress Cataloging in Publication Data

Federal Theatre Project.
  Federal Theatre plays.

  (Franklin D. Roosevelt and the era of the New Deal)
  CONTENTS: Staff of the Living newspaper. Triple-A
plowed under.—Arent, A. Power.—Sundgaard,
A. Spirochete.
  1. American drama—20th century. I. Rohan, Pierre de,
ed. II. Triple-A plowed under. 1973. III. Arent, Arthur.
Power. 1973. IV. Sundgaard, Arnold. Spirochete, a history.
1973. V. Title. VI. Series.
PS634.F4   1973   812'.5'208   72-2386
ISBN 0-306-70494-3

This Da Capo Press edition of *Federal Theatre Plays*
is an unabridged republication of the first edition
published in New York in 1938. It is reprinted by
special arrangement with Random House, Inc.

Copyright, 1938, by Random House, Inc.

Published by Da Capo Press, Inc.
A Subsidiary of Plenum Publishing Corporation
227 West 17th Street, New York, New York 10011

All Rights Reserved

Manufactured in the United States of America

63946

FEDERAL THEATRE PLAYS

Triple-A Plowed Under

Power

Spirochete

FEDERAL THEATRE PLAYS

1 Triple-A Plowed Under

BY THE STAFF OF THE
LIVING NEWSPAPER

2 Power A LIVING NEWSPAPER

BY ARTHUR ARENT

3 Spirochete A HISTORY

BY ARNOLD SUNDGAARD

Federal Theatre project

RANDOM HOUSE · New York · PUBLISHERS

EDITED FOR THE FEDERAL THEATRE
BY PIERRE DE ROHAN

CONTENTS

INTRODUCTION

In the summer of 1935, after Mr. Harry Hopkins, in accordance with the spirit of the Relief Act passed by Congress, had taken the position that unemployed theatre workers should be given a chance to work again, I asked Elmer Rice to take the directorship of the Federal Theatre for New York City. Although he was interested in the plan for a Government-sponsored theatre, and although he was undismayed by the fears deterring a number of other theatrical people, namely, that the relief rolls would afford little theatrical talent, and that the one dollar out of every ten allowed for all other-than-labor costs would be too small for adequate productions, he hesitated.

"What could we do with all the actors?" he kept saying. "Even if we had twenty plays in rehearsal at once, with thirty in a cast, that would keep only a fraction of them busy." Not wanting to lose Elmer Rice, I snatched at a straw. "We wouldn't use them all in plays—we could do Living Newspapers. We could dramatize the news with living actors, light, music, movement." Elmer Rice caught the idea in the air. "I can get the Newspaper Guild to back it." Acting with his usual velocity once his mind was made up, he accepted the directorship for New York, secured the sponsorship of the Guild, and appointed Morris Watson to head the Living Newspaper company.

The staff of the Living Newspaper was set up like a large city daily, with editor-in-chief, managing editor, city editor, reporters and copyreaders, and they began, as Brooks Atkinson later remarked, "to shake the living daylights out of a thousand books, reports, newspaper and magazine articles," in order to evolve an authoritative dramatic treatment, at once historic and contemporary, of current problems. With Arthur Arent as editor and later as playwright, the Living Newspaper from the first was concerned not with surface news, scandal, human interest stories, but rather with the conditions back of conditions.

For the first Living Newspaper we decided on *Ethiopia,* partly because it was the big news of the moment, and partly because we had a large group of Negro dancers and actors on our project. By November the research was complete, the script ready, rehearsals under way, and the Biltmore Theatre the rendezvous for directors, actors and writers interested in the new form.

Then something happened which was to have a profound bearing not only on the Living Newspaper, but on the entire history of the Federal Theatre. The State Department heard of the play, became concerned, and there was transmitted through my administrative superior, Mr. Jacob Baker, an order that no dramatic representation could be made upon any Federal Theatre stage of any living foreign ruler. We explained that the scenes showing Mussolini and Haile Selassie were factual and not caricatured in any way. We were assured that on any American subject we would have freedom of expression, but that the actual portrayal of foreign rulers might involve our diplomatic relations. Elmer Rice, because he believed that this action prophesied that we could never do any socially valuable play, resigned under dramatic circumstances, making his reasons known in a speech given before an invited audience of newspaper men at a private showing of the banned play on January 24, 1936.

Great as was the loss of Elmer Rice to the Federal Theatre, his protest against censorship has been a potent factor in keeping that theatre, in spite of various local fights, some of which we have lost, close to the line laid down by Harry Hopkins when at its inception he said that it was to be "a free, adult, uncensored theatre."

The best proof of that fact may be found in the plays in this volume.

Every Living Newspaper has been different in history and technique, and every one has been exciting to produce. During the rehearsals of *Triple-A Plowed Under* we had one night a rebellion of some of the actors who sent word by the stage manager that they did not want to appear in this kind of performance. Philip Barber, director for New York, Morris Watson, Arthur Arent, Joe Losey and Gordon Graham, the directors, and I met with them after the rehearsal and listened to impassioned speeches explaining why this swift, pantomimic, monosyllabic, factual document was not drama and why no New York audience would sit through it. They complained that there was no plot, no story, no chance to build up a character, no public interest in the subject matter. "Who in New York cares about the farmer, about wheat, about the price of bread and milk?"

After they spoke from the floor, those of us who believed in the Living Newspaper—and this included some members of the company—had a chance to tell them that we realized that we were taking a long shot, but that we thought we must take long shots if the Federal Theatre was to succeed. In addition to the production of classics, modern plays, vaudeville and variety, children's plays and dance plays, we felt we should experiment with new forms, particularly because we wished to supplement and stimulate, rather than to compete with commercial Broadway productions. We argued that people today are interested in facts, as proved by the enormous increase in circulation of newspapers and news sheets and by the *March of Time*. We urged the actors to withhold judgment as to the effectiveness of the play until we added two powerful elements which were an intrinsic part of the plan, the musical score and the light score. We ended with a mutual agreement: the actors were to give us all they had through the first performance; if the play failed we promised to drop all plans for future Living Newspapers. We then proceeded to screw our courage to the sticking point, and we had need of it, for the last days of rehearsal were hectic. It was reported that an organization calling itself the World War Veterans threatened to close the show on the ground that it was unpatriotic. Rumor ran through the project that the curtain would never be allowed to rise, that the performers would be hauled off the stage and into patrol wagons. Opening night found the actors full of misgivings, the audience full of tension, and the lobby full of police.

The danger point was a line by Earl Browder—not, as Heywood Broun later carefully explained, really Earl Browder, but merely an actor representing Earl Browder. At this juncture an irate gentleman arose in the back of the house, and in stentorian tones started singing the *Star-Spangled Banner,* demanding that the audience join him. The police who had been warned by the Veterans'·Association to be on guard against Communist activities evidently misunderstood the nature of the song and promptly ejected the gentleman. The play went on; not only on that night but through many succeeding months, not only in New York, but later in Chicago, San Francisco, Cleveland and Los Angeles.

In *Power,* the struggle inherent in all Living Newspapers becomes, through the character of the Consumer, more explicit. It is the struggle of the average citizen to understand the natural, social and economic forces around him, and to achieve through these forces, a better life for more people. If you think such a struggle is undramatic, reserve judgment until, through the roaring waterfalls and vast

machines of *Power,* you see the torchlight procession of
workers and hear them sing:

> "Oh, see them boys a-comin'
> Their Government they trust,
> Just hear their hammers ringin',
> They'll build that dam or bust!"

Critics, who had hitherto accused us of biting the hand
that fed us, now accused us of licking that hand. As a
matter of fact, we were doing neither. We were producing
a play which seemed to us dramatic. The public apparently
shared that belief. Sixty thousand people considered the
theme dramatic enough to buy seats for *Power* before it
opened its sensational New York run.

Melodrama? Of course. Like all so-called new forms the
Living Newspaper borrows with fine impartiality from
many sources: from Aristophanes, from the *Commedia dell'
Arte,* from Shakespearean soliloquy, from the pantomime
of Mei Lan Fang. Being a flexible technique and only in its
beginning, it still has much to learn from the chorus, the
camera, the cartoon. Although it has occasional reference
to the *Volksbühne* and the Blue Blouses, to Bragaglia and
Meierhold and Eisenstein, it is as American as Walt Dis-
ney, the *March of Time* and the *Congressional Record,* to
all of which American institutions it is indebted. Any technical discussion of its diverse elements—factual and formal,
musical and acrobatic, abstract and concrete, visual and
audible, psychological, economic, and social—forms the
subject, not for an introduction, but for a later volume.

In the meantime it is not to be imagined that New
York has a monopoly on the Living Newspaper, or that
Ethiopia, 1935, Triple-A Plowed Under, Power and *One-
Third of a Nation* tell the story. Not only are these New
York editions re-enacted in many other cities, but Oregon

has its own Living Newspaper on *Flax,* Iowa on *Dirt,* Newark on the history of the Negro. Denver is writing one on the sugar-beet industry, and Cincinnati on *Flood Control.*

In *Spirochete,* Arnold Sundgaard, a writer of the Chicago Federal Theatre, tells in Living Newspaper form the story of the fight against syphilis, tells it with such effect that the daily press, *Variety,* and *Billboard,* report it as sensational entertainment, while Paul de Kruif and the Assistant Surgeon General of the United States enlist its service in the nationwide struggle against the disease, even the nameless mention of which once put Ibsen in the pillory.

All of which seems to indicate that the truth is not only stranger but often more entertaining and more dramatically effective than fiction. In fact, this conclusion might be said to apply to the entire history of the Federal Theatre.

HALLIE FLANAGAN,
Director, Federal Theatre

Washington, D. C.
May 11, 1938

TRIPLE-A PLOWED UNDER

A Living Newspaper

Sponsored by
The Newspaper Guild of America

*Written by the Editorial Staff of the Living Newspaper
Under the Supervision of Arthur Arent*

ALFRED E. SMITH AND THE SUPREME COURT SILHOUETTED AGAINST
THE CONSTITUTION OF THE UNITED STATES

Federal Theatre Photo by Richard Rose

Triple-A Plowed Under was first produced by the Federal Theatre Project at the Biltmore Theatre on March 14, 1936, with the following cast:

Voice of the Living Newspaper—William Randolph, Jr.
1. The Living Newspaper Overture
2. Triple-A Plowed Under

Scene One—*War and Inflation*

First Speaker	Bentley Wallace
Second Speaker	Ben Lewis
Woman Speaker	Fay Courteney

Scene Two—*Deflation*

Exporter	Robert Brennan
Jobber	David Leight
City Banker	Charles Danforth
Country Banker	Harry Brooks
Farmer	Burton Mallory

Scene Three—*Vicious Circle*

Farmer	Robert Mack
Dealer	Lionel Dante
Manufacturer	Lawrence Clarke
Worker	Richard Keller

Scene Four—*Farmers' Holiday*

Milo Reno	Edward LeDuc
Pres. of Merchants Assoc.	Guido Alexander
Three Committeemen	

Charles Uday, Ilya Scheffer, Henry Russelli

3

SCENE FIVE—*Milk Prices*

Middleman	Norman Lloyd
Produce Farmer	Robert Noack
Consumer	Marion Day

SCENE SIX—*Farmers Organize*

Chairman	Charles Danforth
Platform Speaker	William Humphrey
Audience Speakers	

    Robert Donaldson, Charles Uday, Eddie Howard, Howard Washburne, Lionel Dante

SCENE SEVEN—*Milk Strike*

Leaders	Burton Mallory, Richey White

SCENE EIGHT—*Farm Auction*

Auctioneer	David Leight
Sheriff	Charles Bunnell
First Bidder	Rickey White
Second Bidder	Walter Palm

SCENE NINE—*Lem Harris, Secretary of the Farmers' National Relief Conference*

Lem Harris	James Bradleigh

SCENE TEN—*Farm and City Families*

Voice of Secy. Wallace	Bentley Wallace
Voice of Hugh S. Johnson	Charles Dill
Worker	Emil Miller
Wife	Fay Courteney
Son	Wade Dent
Daughter	Jane Jonson
Farmer	Burton Mallory
Wife	Gertrude Perry
First Son	Robert Horowitz

Second Son   William Randolph
Daughter   Gloria Sheldon

SCENE ELEVEN—*Birth of Triple-A*

A.—VOICE OF WALLACE

Secretary Wallace   Bentley Wallace
Voice   Raoul Henry

B.—SHIRT SCENE

Farm Bureau Rep.   Eddie Howard
Farmer   Burton Mallory
Shirt Salesman   Norman Lloyd

SCENE TWELVE—*Commodities Skyrocket*

A.—WHEAT PIT

Voice   Lionel Dante

B.—COUNTER RESTAURANT

Counter Man   Ivan Acharg
Customer   Charles Randolph

C.—PARK AVENUE RESTAURANT

Man   Coburne Goodwin
Woman   Eleanora Barrie

SCENE THIRTEEN—*Drought*

A.—FAIR AND WARMER

Farmer   Burton Mallory

B.—CHURCH

Minister   Charles Danforth

C.—WHEAT PIT

SCENE FOURTEEN—*Sharecroppers*

Farmer   Jules Ferrar
Sharecroppers
    Robert Noack, Jack Denver, Robert Horowitz and
    Raoul Henry

6   TRIPLE-A PLOWED UNDER

Scene Fifteen—*Detroit Meat Strike*

Customer	André Dumont
Leader of Women	Jean Bauer
Pickets, Shoppers, Pedestrians	

Scene Sixteen—*The Sherwood Case*

Police Lieutenant	James Bradleigh
Mrs. Dorothy Sherwood	Jane Jonson
Police Officer	Armin Bekaffy

Scene Seventeen—*Supreme Court*

Speaker for Majority	Norman Lloyd
Speaker for Minority	James Bradleigh
Senator Daniel O. Hastings	Wilbur De Rouge
Alfred E. Smith	Rickey White
Earl Browder	William Humphrey
Thomas Jefferson	Burton Mallory

Scene Eighteen—*The Big "Steal"*

Secretary Wallace	Bentley Wallace

Scene Nineteen—*Soil Conservation*

Secretary Davis	Robert Brennan
First Reporter	David Leight
Second Reporter	Guido Alexander
Secretary	Eddie Howard

Scene Twenty—*Finale of TRIPLE-A PLOWED UNDER*

Staged by Joe Losey
Associate Director, H. Gordon Graham

Settings by Hjalmar Hermanson

Costumes Designed by   Kathryn Wilson

Music by Lee Wainer
Produced under the Supervision of Morris Watson

The Living Newspaper Theatre Orchestra
Myron Roman, Conductor
Federal Music Project

(NOTE: *As a matter of convenience, scene groupings were altered slightly for the New York City production.*)

SCENE ONE
(War and Inflation) *

CHARACTERS

VOICE OF LIVING NEWSPAPER
LINE OF SOLDIERS
TABLEAU OF FARMERS
FIRST MAN
SECOND MAN
WOMAN, middle-aged, prosperous

(*As overture ends, voice over the* LOUDSPEAKER *speaks.*)
VOICE OF LIVING NEWSPAPER (*over* LOUDSPEAKER): Triple-A
Plowed Under. (*Curtain rises*) 1917—Inflation.
(*At rise red spotlight is on* SOLDIERS *marching in continuous columns up ramp placed upstage left. After a brief interval there is an increasing volume of marching feet. The entire scene is played behind scrim. Spotlight on three* SPEAKERS *and crowd of* FARMERS. SPEAKERS *stand on highest level, right. Some of the* FARMERS *stand on lowest level, right, and some at stage level, right.*)
FIRST SPEAKER: Your country is at war.
SECOND SPEAKER: Your country needs you.
FIRST AND SECOND SPEAKERS (*together*): If you can't fight—
farm.
FIRST SPEAKER: The fate of our country rests upon the
farmers.
SECOND SPEAKER: Do you want our land invaded?
FIRST SPEAKER: Do you want your daughters ravaged by
Huns?

* Based on communications between Hallie Flanagan, Director, Federal Theatre Project, and Paul H. Appleby, Dept. of Agriculture, Washington, D. C., February 12 and 13, 1936.

WOMAN: Farmer, save the nation! (*Trumpet.*)

FIRST SPEAKER: The boys in the trenches need the men in the fields.

WOMAN: Farmer, save our boys. (*Trumpet.*)

SECOND SPEAKER: Every bushel of barley is a barrel of bullets.

WOMAN: Farmer, save democracy. (*Trumpet.*)

FIRST SPEAKER: Every hand with a spade is a hand-grenade.

WOMAN: Farmer, save our honor. (*Trumpet.*)

SECOND SPEAKER: Every man behind a plow is a man behind a gun.

WOMAN: Farmer, save civilization. (*Trumpet.*)

FIRST SPEAKER: Every head of cattle can win a battle.

WOMAN: Farmer, save our flag. (*Trumpet.*)

FIRST SPEAKER: Plant more wheat.

SECOND SPEAKER: Plant more potatoes.

FIRST SPEAKER: More corn!

SECOND SPEAKER: More cotton!

FIRST SPEAKER: More food, more seed, more acres!

SECOND AND FIRST SPEAKER (*together*): More! More! More!

WOMAN: Farmer, save the world!

Portals close

SCENE TWO—A
(*Deflation*) *

CHARACTERS

VOICE OF LIVING NEWSPAPER

SUB-SCENE A

AN EXPORTER

A JOBBER

* Based on communications, February 12 and 13, 1936, between Hallie Flanagan, Director, Federal Theatre Project, and Paul H. Appleby, Dept. of Agriculture, Washington, D. C.

SUB-SCENE B
CITY BANKER
COUNTRY BANKER
SUB-SCENE C
COUNTRY BANKER
FARMER

VOICE OF LIVING NEWSPAPER (*over* LOUDSPEAKER): The 1920's. Deflation.

(*This scene is played in a series of three sub-scenes, on three levels. The highest level is stage right, the intermediate level, center, and the lowest level, left. First scene on highest level is lighted from directly overhead. Only the scene actually playing is lighted. Blackout at the end of each scene, as the spotlight comes up on the next scene. Chart indicating deflation is projected on scrim throughout this series.*)

EXPORTER: Bad news, Frank. I can't ship any more of your wheat.

JOBBER: What will I do with my stocks?

EXPORTER: I don't know! I can't ship any more to Europe— the war's over.

JOBBER: It's been over a long time, but they still need to eat, don't they?

EXPORTER: Yes, but they're raising their own. I'm afraid we won't ship much more wheat to Europe unless they have another war.

JOBBER: That's a short explanation of a serious problem.

EXPORTER: Well, anyway, you see why I can't take your shipment.

JOBBER: I don't see a damn thing.

Blackout

SCENE TWO—B

(Spotlight comes up on middle level, CITY BANKER *seated at desk,* COUNTRY BANKER *standing at his side, left.)*

CITY BANKER *(as if there had been a previous conversation)*: It's just good banking, that's the only answer I can give you.

COUNTRY BANKER: It may be good banking for you fellows here in the city, but I tell you that if I pay up all my paper now I've got to bankrupt every farmer in my district.

CITY BANKER: I'm sorry. I'm not permitted to be concerned over that. I wouldn't be true to my trust if I didn't keep this bank's money in lucrative channels. It just happens that at the moment stock and bond collateral is the safest investment. Besides, we get considerably more returns there.

COUNTRY BANKER: What's going to happen when we bankrupt the farmers? Are you going to eat your stocks and bonds?

CITY BANKER: I have no time for levity, Mr. Brown. The fact is, agriculture is no longer a lucrative investment; stocks and bonds are. Now do you see that I must call in your paper?

COUNTRY BANKER: I don't see a damn thing.

Blackout

SCENE TWO—C

(Spotlight comes up on lowest level, left, COUNTRY BANKER *seated at desk, and* FARMER *seated at his side, right.)*

BANKER *(as if there had been previous conversation)*: I've got to have the money.

FARMER: I can't understand it. Only a little while ago they were preaching and haranguing for us to raise more crops and more crops. Damn it, I bought more land and cleared all the woods on my place, and planted it to wheat, and now it's rotting in the fields.

BANKER: That was war, Fred.

FARMER: Well, hell, people still need to eat, don't they? And they can't tell me there aren't people who couldn't eat what's lying out in my fields now. My son, Jim, in New York says he can't walk down the street without having hungry men beg him for money.

BANKER: Well, I don't see what I can do, unless they ease up on me, and they aren't going to do that.

FARMER: Well, if you foreclose on me I'll be in the bread-line myself. Then how are any of us going to eat?

BANKER: When that happens the big boys will begin to feel it, and maybe they'll get up another war.

FARMER (*grimly*): Can't have another war. Every day I get veterans asking for a handout, and not a one of them would go back to war, and by God, I wouldn't raise wheat for another war.

BANKER: At any rate, you see my situation, Fred.

FARMER: I don't see a damn thing.

Blackout

SCENE THREE

(*Farmer, Dealer, Manufacturer, Worker—Vicious Circle*) *

CHARACTERS

VOICE OF LIVING NEWSPAPER

A FARMER

A DEALER

* Digest of article "A.A.A. Philosophy" by Rexford G. Tugwell, *Fortune Magazine,* January 1934.

A MANUFACTURER

A WORKER

VOICE OF LIVING NEWSPAPER (*over* LOUDSPEAKER): In the troubled fifteen years, 1920 to 1935, farm incomes fall five and one-half billion dollars; * unemployment rises seven million, five hundred and seventy-eight thousand.† (*Four spotlights come up on the four protagonists of this scene.* FARMER, *stage right, turns head sharply left, speaks to* DEALER.)

FARMER (*to* DEALER): I can't buy that auto. (*Light goes out.* DEALER *turns head sharply left, speaks to* MANUFACTURER.)

DEALER (*to* MANUFACTURER): I can't take that shipment. (*Count of one, light out.* MANUFACTURER *turns head sharply left, speaks to* WORKER.)

MANUFACTURER (*to* WORKER): I can't use you any more. (*Light goes out.* WORKER *speaks directly front.*)

WORKER: I can't eat.   (*Light goes out.*)

SCENE FOUR

(*Farmers' Holiday*)

CHARACTERS

VOICE OF LIVING NEWSPAPER

A. MILO RENO

B. MILO RENO

PRESIDENT OF COMMISSION MERCHANTS

THREE COMMISSION MERCHANTS

* a. "The Agricultural Situation"—Bureau of Agricultural Economics. b. Yearbook of Agriculture—1935.

† a. National Bureau of Economic Research. b. National Industrial Conference Board, November 1935.

SCENE FOUR—A

VOICE OF LIVING NEWSPAPER: Des Moines, Iowa. Farmers pin hopes on farm holiday leader, Milo Reno.*
(*Lights on* MILO RENO *on proscenium on right.*)
MILO RENO: As President of the Farmers' Holiday Association, representing five thousand farmers, I wish to announce the five points of our program during the coming strike.

1. We will pay no taxes or interest until we have fully cared for our families.
2. We will pay no interest-bearing debts until we receive the cost of production.
3. We will buy only that which complete necessity demands.
4. We will stay in the homes we now occupy.
5. We will not sell our products until we receive the cost of production, but will exchange our products with labor and the unemployed for the things we need on the farm on the basis of cost of production for both parties.†

You can no more stop this movement than you could stop the Revolution of 1776. I couldn't stop it if I tried.‡
(*Off stage voices shout, "Strike! Strike!" Follow* RENO *with spot to stage left, where light comes up on* COMMISSION MERCHANTS *behind desk. Lights shift to left.*)

* *New York Times,* August 16th and 26th, 1932.
† "Bryan! Bryan! Bryan! Bryan!", *Fortune Magazine,* January 1934, p. 68.
‡ *Seeds of Revolt* by Mauritz A. Hallgren—(Alfred Knopf, 1933).

SCENE FOUR—B

PRESIDENT OF COMMISSION MERCHANTS (*holding out contract and pen to* MILO RENO): Mr. Reno, I have here the terms drawn up by the committee of Commission Merchants. . . . We want you to call off that strike. . . . Will you sign? (*Pause.* MILO RENO *turns to where off stage voices are still rumbling "Strike! Strike!" He turns back, and signs.*)

Blackout

SCENE FIVE
(*Milk Prices*)

CHARACTERS

VOICE OF LIVING NEWSPAPER
MIDDLEMAN
FARMER
CONSUMER, A WOMAN

VOICE OF LIVING NEWSPAPER (*over* LOUDSPEAKER): Milk flows to market.
(*Light directly over the* MIDDLEMAN *seated at table.* FARMER *and* CONSUMER *on truck, right and left of* MIDDLEMAN. *Scene is played on metronome count through entirety, a speech and a beat, etc.*)
FARMER (*holding up quart can of milk*): How much do I get?
MIDDLEMAN: Three cents.*
FARMER: Three cents?
MIDDLEMAN: Take it or leave it.

* *New York Herald Tribune,* July 5, 1934.

FARMER: I'll take it. (*Hands over milk and pockets coins.*)
WOMAN CONSUMER: I want a quart of milk.
MIDDLEMAN (*who has been pouring milk from can into bottle*): Fifteen cents.
WOMAN CONSUMER: Fifteen cents?
MIDDLEMAN: Take it or leave it.
WOMAN CONSUMER: I'll take it. (MIDDLEMAN *holds out his hand, takes money, and slaps pocket.*)

Blackout

SCENE SIX
(*Sioux City—Farmers Organize*)

CHARACTERS

VOICE OF LIVING NEWSPAPER
FIRST SPEAKER
SECOND SPEAKER from audience
THIRD SPEAKER from audience
FOURTH SPEAKER from audience
CHAIRMAN
FIFTH SPEAKER from audience

VOICE OF LIVING NEWSPAPER (*over* LOUDSPEAKER): Sioux City—August 31, 1932—Farmers organize Relief Conference in theatre.*
(*The stage is a speaker's platform.* DELEGATES *are seated in various parts of the lower floor of the theatre.* CHAIRMAN *and* FIRST SPEAKER *are at table on stage.*)
FIRST SPEAKER: We've been sold out! We've been cheated and robbed. Milo Reno declared a holiday for Milo Reno—not for us. Forget Reno. Forget his crazy schemes! For God's sake, think for yourselves. I say, let's organize

* *New York Times,* September 1, 1932.

intelligently.* We've got to solve our problems clean and straight, or there will be those who will solve them with bayonets.†

SECOND SPEAKER (*from audience*): We ain't scared, Mister.

THIRD SPEAKER (*also from audience*): We'll fight if we have to.

CHAIRMAN (*coming down stage a bit*): If anyone wants to speak, let him stand up.

FOURTH SPEAKER (*from audience*): I got something to say.

CHAIRMAN (*nods*).

FOURTH SPEAKER: Men, talk is cheap. . . . Tons and tons of dirt are being thrown at Milo Reno. This is all a stunt to take your mind off the real situation—the milk situation. I say, "Stick to Reno. . . . He meant to . . ." (*Cries of "Boo" from the audience.*) ‡

FOURTH SPEAKER: All right, "Boo" if you want to, but I say you're making a mistake. (*Cries of "Pipe down," "Get off" and "Boo."*)

CHAIRMAN (*holding up hand for silence*): Friends, there's a great deal to be done. Yesterday fourteen of our men were shot down on the picket line in Cherokee County. . . . We want our rights. . . . We want relief . . . and we will get it.§ (*Thunderous roar greets him. Cries of "Strike!" "Dump the milk!" and "Turn over the trucks!"*)

FIFTH SPEAKER (*from audience*): Men! We've got to save ourselves, with or without Milo Reno—and the only way to do that is to dump every truck and spill every can of milk we can lay our hands on. Let's stop talking and *do* something! (*Tremendous roar.*)

Blackout

* *New York Times*, September 1, 1932.
† *Ibid.*, September 4, 1932.
‡ *Ibid.*, September 1, 1932.
§ *Ibid.*

SCENE SEVEN
(*Milk Strike*)

CHARACTERS

VOICE OF LIVING NEWSPAPER
A GROUP OF A DOZEN MEN
FIRST MAN
SECOND MAN
THIRD MAN
VOICE (off stage)

(*During darkness following Scene Six, cries of "Strike" have given way to an ominous musical undercurrent. Throughout this scene, music continues, highlighting the climaxes, but at no time becoming more than a background.*)

VOICE OF LIVING NEWSPAPER (*over* LOUDSPEAKER): The challenge echoes through Wisconsin, Ohio, Iowa, Indiana. Over the Middle West embittered farmers act.*

(*The stage is completely dark save for a faint light which illuminates a crossroad signpost and part of an immense boulder. At rise there is no sound, but after a moment, the faint sound of an approaching truck is heard. This becomes louder and soon the twin lights of automobile headlights appear left. They grow stronger as the auto comes nearer, and sound increases. The lights have by this time reached the boulder, lighting up the heads of a* DOZEN MEN *grouped around and behind it, men who have been lying in wait to waylay the truck. As the lights hit them, one speaks:*)

FIRST MAN: Here comes the truck, boys.

SECOND MAN: Let's get it.

* *New York Times*, August 16, 1932.

THIRD MAN (*stopping him with his hand*): Wait. (*There is a second's pause as the lights get brighter.*)

SECOND MAN: Now! (*The* MEN *leap out from behind the boulder and rush off left. A single voice is heard off stage—clearly—with great but quiet determination.*)

VOICE OFF STAGE: Get down off that truck. . . . (*There is a split-second pause.*)

TWO OR THREE VOICES: Dump the milk! * (*From off stage is heard the ripping and smashing of boxes being hurled from the truck. . . . A moment of this and then one voice, clear and loud.*)

VOICE: Turn over the truck. Push! (*A moment . . . then the final terrific crash as the truck is turned over.*)

Blackout

(NOTE: *This effect is heightened by the following device: as the truck is being turned over, the lights on the boulder swing round dizzily until, instead of being one beside the other, they have become one over the other. . . . There is a full second's pause as they remain in that position, before the blackout.*)

SCENE EIGHT
(*Farm Auction*)

CHARACTERS

VOICE OF LIVING NEWSPAPER
AUCTIONEER
SHERIFF
FIRST NEIGHBOR
OWNER (FRED)
SON (WILSON)

* Article by Bruce Bliven, *New Republic*, November 29, 1933.

JOHN
THIRD NEIGHBOR
ALBERT
FARMERS, MEN AND WOMEN
STRANGER

VOICE OF LIVING NEWSPAPER (*over* LOUDSPEAKER): Farmers lose their land—their homes—unpaid mortgages are foreclosed; land is sold at public auction. The farmers take matters in their own hands.*

(*The scene is a farmyard, but there is no attempt at realism; blue cyclorama, gray platform for auctioneer, barrel on platform. Gray ground row to mask lights on floor in front of eye. Otherwise no further properties in scene.* FARMERS *are in overalls, a few* WOMEN *in crowd. One* MAN *conspicuous in business clothes stands apart. All this is discovered at rise. The time is clearly afternoon, the day bright.*)

FIRST NEIGHBOR (*beckoning*): Hey, Sam! Albert's going to do the talkin'. John'll speak up first.

WILSON: † There's a fellow here I don't know.

FRED: He was asking me questions about the place.

FIRST NEIGHBOR: Point him out, Sam, and I'll watch. (WILSON *nods his head backward toward a well-dressed man, who is walking about. The* MAN *finally stops in front of a group of farmers, and engages them in casual conversation.*)

STRANGER: Nice day for an auction. (*The* GROUP OF FARMERS *look at him in disgust, turn away.* STRANGER *shrugs shoulder, and turns to* FIRST *and* SECOND NEIGHBOR *standing near.*)

AUCTIONEER: We're all ready, folks, soon's the sheriff reads his notice. (SHERIFF *reads in an unintelligible fast mono-*

* *Literary Digest,* January 21, 1933.
† Fictional character.

tone, "State of Wisconsin . . ." WILSON goes through
GROUP OF FARMERS, from person to person, speaking so
that the audience can hear.)

WILSON: Albert's going to do the rest of the talkin'. (Each
FARMER nods in understanding manner. WILSON continues
as he reaches JOHN) You speak up first. Albert'll do the
talkin'. (As SHERIFF completes his reading of the notice,
the AUCTIONEER comes down with his hammer.)

AUCTIONEER: Folks, today you're going to be able to buy
a lot of up-to-date modern machinery, and the best piece
of farm land this side of the Mississippi River, and I
want to see some spirited bidding. (FARMERS watch him
grimly and silently) The valuation of the farm alone is
twenty thousand dollars, three hundred acres under cultivation. Lock, stock and barrel, I should say it's worth,
conservatively speakin', thirty thousand dollars. I leave it
to you, gents, as to how we bid. All to oncet, or piece
by piece? What'dya say we keep the pikers out. . . .
(Meaningly, to STRANGER) All to oncet. (STRANGER nods
slightly. FARMERS all turn their heads in unison toward
STRANGER who is still occupied by two farmers talking to
him) . . . Any objection? (There is no answer) . . .
All right, thirty thousand dollars on the block. What am
I bid? (Slight pause.)

JOHN (quietly, unemotionally): Twelve cents.*
(Pause. FARMERS remain grimly silent.)

AUCTIONEER (forcing a laugh): That's a good one. Twelve
cents. . . . Ha! Ha! Well, now, let's have a bid!

JOHN: That's my bid. (AUCTIONEER looks around and is
sobered by the dead earnestness of the FARMERS. His next
speech, in dead earnestness likewise, is spoken meaning-
fully, directly to the stranger.)

AUCTIONEER: All right, I've got a bid. I'm bid twelve cents

* New York Times, February 2, 1933.

on thirty thousand dollars' worth of property, twelve cents. (*Right at* STRANGER) Who'll bid a thousand? Do I hear a thousand? (STRANGER *opens his mouth to speak. He starts to raise his arm. The* FIRST NEIGHBOR *grabs his hand.* THIRD NEIGHBOR *spins him around, tips his hat over his eyes and the two lead him off,* THIRD NEIGHBOR *speaking.*)

THIRD NEIGHBOR: . . . and when it rains around these parts, Mister, it pours. And you ought to see the pigs down to my place. It's the likeliest litter of little devils anybody ever seen. (*His voice trails off as they disappear off stage. The auctioneer's jaw sags. He looks at the* SHERIFF *and tries to catch his glance.* SHERIFF *deliberately turns his back and starts whittling.*)

JOHN: Whattya waitin' for? You got a bid.

AUCTIONEER: All right. Twelve cents, twelve cents, what do I hear? I've got to have another bid. 'Tain't legal less I have another bid.

ALBERT: Thirteen cents. (*Dead pause. The* AUCTIONEER *looks beaten, as if he hadn't heard the bid*) You got your bid. (*There is another, shorter pause, during which the* AUCTIONEER *looks more helpless than ever*) Well, whattaya waitin' for? Call it!

AUCTIONEER (*thoroughly licked, smacks his hammer down hard*): All right, thirteen cents once . . . thirteen cents twice . . . thirteen cents. . . . Are you all done? Sold for thirteen cents.

Blackout

SCENE NINE

(*Lem Harris, Secretary of the Farmers' National Relief Conference*)

CHARACTERS

VOICE OF LIVING NEWSPAPER
LEM HARRIS

VOICE OF LIVING NEWSPAPER (*over* LOUDSPEAKER): Washington, December 7th, 1932. (*Music*) And so it gives me great pleasure to introduce to the delegates of the Farmers' National Relief Conference, your secretary, Mr. Lem Harris.*

(*Applause; spot up on* LEM HARRIS *down stage left, speaking over microphone.*)

LEM HARRIS: The farmers themselves have come here to Washington to frame their own proposals for immediate relief from the burdens under which they are now being crushed. In their opinion a national emergency exists, and this is a time for emergency action. That means immediate relief, not some complicated scheme to "make the tariff effective" several years hence. (*Pause*) The three-quarters of the farmers, which economists consider as surplus, cannot really be considered as such. Neither can they consider their crops as surplus when they know that there are millions of unemployed who lack the very things which they produce and cannot sell. It was the recognition of this ironical situation which led the farmers of Iowa to give milk to the unemployed of Sioux City during the farm strike there. Remember, every farmer coming to this Conference has had personal experience with the farm problem, he is a real dirt farmer, elected

* *New York Times*, December 8, 1932, *et supra*.

by at least twenty-five farmers back home. His coming
spells the distrust of the professional farm lobbies. He
has taken matters into his own hands because he knows
that no one else can do the job as well as he can.*

Blackout

SCENE TEN †
(*Farm and City Families*)

CHARACTERS

VOICE OF LIVING NEWSPAPER
GENERAL HUGH S. JOHNSON'S VOICE
CITY GROUP
    WORKER
    WORKER'S WIFE
    WORKER'S FIRST SON
    WORKER'S SECOND SON
    WORKER'S DAUGHTER
FARM GROUP
    FARMER
    FARMER'S WIFE
    FARMER'S FIRST SON
    FARMER'S SECOND SON
    FARMER'S DAUGHTER

VOICE OF LIVING NEWSPAPER (*over* LOUDSPEAKER): As our
economic system now works, the greater the surplus of
wheat on Nebraska farms, the larger are the breadlines
in New York City.
(*As curtains open on brilliant blue glass curtain, against
it are seen silhouetted a farm and city family, the city*

* *Ibid.*, December 11, 1932.
† Creative—digest of news.

family, center, and the farm family right, on ramp. The
scene grows angry as the two groups oppose each other.)

WORKER: We starve and they told us you had food in your
fields.

FARMER: Food is in our fields but they told us you would
not pay the cost of its harvesting.

WORKER'S WIFE: We had no money.

FARMER'S FIRST SON: We raised eggs and milk, and you
wouldn't buy them.

WORKER'S FIRST SON: We had not the fifteen cents to pay.

FARMER'S FAMILY (*aroused*): Fifteen cents for milk?

FARMER: We got only three.

WORKER'S FAMILY (*shouting*): Fifteen, fifteen!

FARMER'S FAMILY: Three, three!

WORKER'S DAUGHTER (*wail*): I'm hungry. . . .

FARMER'S DAUGHTER: I can't go to school. . . .

FARMER (*quietly*): Food rots in our fields. . . .

FARMER'S SECOND SON: No money to ship. . . .

FARMER: No money to buy. . . .

FARMER'S WIFE: No money . . . (*Slight pause.*)

WORKER: There is no work.

WORKER'S SON: No jobs!

WORKER'S DAUGHTER: No food!

WORKER: We have been evicted from our homes.

FARMER'S WIFE: And we from our land.

FARMER: We plow our sweat into the earth.

FARMER'S WIFE: And bring forth ripe provender.

WORKER: We starve.

FARMER: The wheat stands high in our fields.

FARMER'S WIFE: *Our* fields no longer.

WORKER'S DAUGHTER: Feed us.

FARMER'S FIRST SON: Pay us.

WORKER'S FAMILY: Feed us.

FARMER: The wheat is better destroyed. I say, burn it!

FARMER'S FAMILY: Burn it! Burn it!

(*Flame lights up, changing the sky from blue to red. Against the flames is silhouetted the figure of a farmer in shadow, holding a pitchfork. Farm and city families hold this tableau, all through speech of* GENERAL JOHNSON *over the* LOUDSPEAKER.)

WORKER: Why?

VOICE OF GENERAL JOHNSON (*over* LOUDSPEAKER): Something is depriving one-third of our population of the God-given right to earn their bread by the sweat of their labor. That single ugly fact is an indictment under which no form of government can long continue. For slighter causes than that we revolted against British rule, and suffered the bitterest civil war in history.*

FARMER AND WORKER (*together*): Words! (*Both* FAMILIES *turn in protest toward the* LOUDSPEAKER.)

Close Travelers

SCENE ELEVEN
(*Triple-A Enacted*)

CHARACTERS

VOICE OF LIVING NEWSPAPER
SECRETARY OF AGRICULTURE HENRY A. WALLACE

VOICE OF LIVING NEWSPAPER (*over* LOUDSPEAKER): Washington, May 12th, 1933—the AAA becomes the law of the land. It is hereby declared to be the policy of Congress. . .†

(*Spotlight on* SECRETARY WALLACE.)

SECRETARY WALLACE (*picking up sentence*): . . . to increase

---

* *New York Times,* May 13, 1933.
† *Vital Speeches,* October 21, 1935.

the purchasing power of farmers. It is, by that token, farm relief, but also, by the same token, National Relief, for it is a well-known fact that millions of urban unemployed will have a better chance of going to work when farm purchasing power rises enough to buy the products of city factories. Let's help the farmer. . . . It is trying to subdue the habitual anarchy of a major American industry, and to establish organized control in the interest of not only the farmer but everybody else. . . . The bill gives the Secretary of Agriculture the power to . . .*
(*Lights fade on* WALLACE. *The projection of a map of the United States, showing acreage reduction, comes up on the scrim.*)

VOICE OVER LOUDSPEAKER (*staccato*): . . . Reduce acreage. The visible supply of wheat diminished from two hundred and twelve million bushels in 1932 to one hundred and twenty-four million bushels in 1934.†
(*The projection changes to a number of little pigs in front of a number of large pigs, labeled "1933 production," the smaller pigs labeled "1934 production."*)

VOICE OVER LOUDSPEAKER (*continuing*): To curtail production. Hog production was cut from sixty million in 1933 to thirty-seven million in 1935.†
(*Projection changes to a slide depicting two loaves of bread. One is labeled "1933—10¢" the other "1934—11¢."*) ‡

VOICE OVER LOUDSPEAKER (*continuing*): To levy a tax on processing of basic farm commodities. Wheat advanced in price from 32 cents a bushel in 1933 to 74 cents a bushel in 1934.†

Blackout

* Radio Speech—Farm and Home Hour—WJZ—March 18, 1933.
† *World Almanac*, 1936, pp. 352, 356, 365; *Ibid.*, 1934, p. 347.
‡ Ward Baking Company, New York, N. Y.

SCENE TWELVE
(*Shirt Scene*)

CHARACTERS

VOICE OF LIVING NEWSPAPER
FARM BUREAU REPRESENTATIVE
FARMER
SHIRT SALESMAN

VOICE OF LIVING NEWSPAPER (*over* LOUDSPEAKER): Triple-A pays four million dollars daily.*
(*Three spots directly overhead, stage right, center and stage left, light up as portals open.* FARMER *walks into spot right where he meets* FARM BUREAU REPRESENTATIVE.)

FARM BUREAU REPRESENTATIVE †: Check for reducing wheat acreage.

FARMER: Thanks, I need it. (FARM BUREAU REPRESENTATIVE *exits right,* FARMER *turns front in area of center spot.* SALESMAN *enters left, and* FARMER *and* SALESMAN *meet in area spot left. As* FARM BUREAU REPRESENTATIVE *and* FARMER *vacate spot right, that spot blacks; as* FARMER *vacates spot center, that spot blacks. The entire scene is played crisply, with no attempt at realism*) Got a shirt?

SALESMAN: You bet.

FARMER: How much?

SALESMAN: One dollar.‡

FARMER: It was seventy-five cents.

SALESMAN: Cotton's up—production's curtailed—there's a processing tax.

* *New York Times,* September 17, 1934.
† Fictional character.
‡ Letter from William V. Lawson, Cotton and Textile Institute, 320 Broadway, New York, N. Y.

FARMER: What's it mean?

SALESMAN: You get check for planting no wheat—planter gets check for planting no cotton—planter pays more for bread of your wheat—you pay more for shirt of his cotton—that's where it comes from.

FARMER: Oh, well—when it was cheap I didn't have any money. I'll take it.

Blackout

SCENE THIRTEEN
(*Wheat Pit*)

CHARACTERS

> VOICE OF LIVING NEWSPAPER
> FOUR TELEPHONE MEN
> SEVERAL RUNNERS
> MAN AT BLACKBOARD
> TWO GROUPS OF TRADERS—15 RIGHT, 15 LEFT

VOICE OF LIVING NEWSPAPER (*over* LOUDSPEAKER): Chicago, 1934.

(*The scene is a stylized representation of the Chicago Wheat Pit. Two ramps, their large ends set upstage, are joined by two four-foot platforms. Behind the platforms, elevated, is a blackboard; so that they can be seen over the small ends of the ramps, are open telephone booths. A large clock is next to the blackboard, right. Instead of numerals it depicts the months of the year. It has only one hand. This hand revolves slowly through the playing of the scene. Left of the blackboard is a large thermometer—to indicate increasing heat. The thermometer does not move in this scene.*

There is a MAN *at each of the four telephones, and several*

RUNNERS *between them and the men in the Pit. The Wheat Pit is filled with 30* TRADERS. *These* TRADERS *are divided into groups, left and right, one buying and one selling. At rise there is a din of voices. Immediately after rise a loud gong rings. The two* GROUPS OF TRADERS *speak in unison, those buying speak first, and those selling afterward. Their movements also are in unison—a movement which should be divided on a count of two beats to a measure or four beats to a measure, building tempo and volume of scene consistently until end. Right after gong is sounded,* VOICE OVER LOUDSPEAKER *speaks.*)

VOICE: Triple-A enacted.

(*This same* VOICE *speaks throughout the scene, with a slightly increasing tempo. One* MAN *at blackboard continues his motions of writing through the scene.*)

TRADERS LEFT: Buying 500 May at 101.*

TRADERS RIGHT: Selling 500 May at a quarter.

TRADERS LEFT: Buying 500 May at 101.

TRADERS RIGHT: Selling at a quarter.

TRADERS LEFT: One.

VOICE OVER LOUDSPEAKER: Fair and warmer.†

TRADERS LEFT: Selling at one-eighth.

TRADERS RIGHT: A half.

LOUDSPEAKER (*crisply*): Fair and warmer.

Blackout

* *Journal of Commerce,* December 8 and 22, 1934.

† *New York Times,* August 12, 1934. Weather Bureau reports 1934 thus far driest and hottest on record.

SCENE FOURTEEN *
(*Counter Restaurant*)

CHARACTERS

COUNTERMAN
CUSTOMER

(*As portals close on Wheat Pit, trucks move in right with counter.* COUNTERMAN *stands right of counter, appropriately dressed,* CUSTOMER *left of counter. Light from overhead. Bowl and ladle on counter.* CUSTOMER *very shabbily dressed, with hat over his eyes.*)

COUNTERMAN: Whadd'ya want?
CUSTOMER: A bowl o' oatmeal.
COUNTERMAN: Got three cents?
CUSTOMER: Got two cents.
COUNTERMAN: Not a chance. Got to have three cents.
CUSTOMER: It was two cents yesterday.
COUNTERMAN: Sorry, pal, prices went up today.

Blackout

SCENE FIFTEEN
(*Park Avenue Restaurant*)

CHARACTERS

MAN IN EVENING CLOTHES
WOMAN IN EVENING CLOTHES
WAITER

(*Front light on Restaurant. Background suggests a modern room. A* COUPLE *in evening clothes are seated*

* Creative.

at table. WAITER *is taking the order. They are drinking cocktails.*)

MAN: . . . Imported Beluga caviar. Broiled royal squab, grilled mushrooms and a bottle of Château Yquem, '26. That's all for now.

(*Exit* WAITER.)

WOMAN: Mmmmmmmmmmmm . . . celebrating?

MAN: Right.

WOMAN (*lifts glass*): What to?

MAN: Wheat.

WOMAN: Wheat?

MAN: Wheat.

WOMAN: All right. . . . Here's to wheat. (*They drink.*) Long may it wave.

MAN: And keep going up.

WOMAN (*after a short pause*): Tell me, are you affected by these new processing taxes?

MAN: Uh-huh.

WOMAN: You seem pretty cheerful about it.

MAN: Why shouldn't I, it's the consumer who pays. (*As she looks at him inquiringly, he picks up roll.*) When I buy this roll I pay the processing tax.

WOMAN: I thought you paid it on wheat and hogs and things like that.

MAN: Look, this roll, not so long ago, was wheat waving in the fields of Kansas. Somewhere between the harvesting of that wheat and this roll there was a processing tax. . . . (*He stops.*)

WOMAN: Go on.

MAN: That's all . . . and it's the man who eats it who pays it.

WOMAN (*also after a slight pause*): I'm afraid it's just a bit complicated—for me.

MAN: Oh, well, wheat's up and I've been saving a lot of it to unload. . . . So what will it be, a new car or a sable coat?

WOMAN: Mmmmmmmmmm!
MAN: O.K. Both.

Blackout

SCENE SIXTEEN
(*Drought*)

CHARACTERS

VOICE OF LIVING NEWSPAPER
A FARMER
FIRST VOICE
SECOND VOICE

VOICE OF LIVING NEWSPAPER (*over* LOUDSPEAKER): Summer, 1934: Drought sears the Midwest, West, Southwest.*
(*Light up on tableau of a* FARMER *examining the soil; a sun-baked plain, stretching away to a burning horizon. From the* LOUDSPEAKER *two voices are heard, one crisp, sharp, staccato—the other sinister and foreboding. The* VOICES *are accompanied by a rhythmic musical procession that grows in intensity, and leaps to a climax of shrill despair.*)

FIRST VOICE (*over* LOUDSPEAKER): May first, Midwest weather report.

SECOND VOICE (*over* LOUDSPEAKER): Fair and warmer.

FIRST VOICE: May second, Midwest weather report.

SECOND VOICE: Fair and warmer.

FIRST VOICE: May third, Midwest weather report.

SECOND VOICE: Fair and warmer.

FIRST VOICE: May fourth, Midwest weather report.

SECOND VOICE: Fair and warmer. Fair and warmer. Fair and warmer. Fair and warmer. (*The* FARMER *who is examin-*

* *New York Times,* August 12, 1934.

ing the soil straightens up and slowly lets a handful of dry dust sift through his fingers.)

FARMER: Dust!

Close Travelers

SCENE SEVENTEEN
(Church)

CHARACTERS

PASTOR

VOICE OVER LOUDSPEAKER

VOICE OF LIVING NEWSPAPER

VOICE FROM CONGREGATION—OFF STAGE

(Light on PASTOR *standing at lectern, center and raised about eight feet. This is backed by Gothic church window. The scene is played through scrim. The* PASTOR *is praying as scene begins. Throughout this prayer, off stage voices are heard saying: "Fair and warmer, fair and warmer, fair and warmer.")*

PASTOR: O God, heavenly Father, look down upon thy people. See our plight today. There are those who claim to be children of God, and yet manifest no real heart in the welfare of others. Help us, Almighty Father, where these others fail.*

VOICES FROM CONGREGATION *(fervently)*: Amen!

PASTOR: Our land, already stricken with depression, now suffers from heat and drought, and this is the fourth month of our affliction. From Mississippi to the Rockies our country lies under the searing blast. Our great state has been burned dry. The showers of dust come in clouds so dense as to obscure the midday sun. The corn

* *New York Times,* July 1, 1934.

crumbles to dust at the touch of our hand, and the stalks lie dried and curling in the heat. O God, heavenly Father, who has blessed the earth that it might be fruitful and bring forth whatsoever is needful for the life of man, and has commanded us to work with quietness, and eat our own bread, bless the labors of the husbandmen . . . (*Projection of film of dying cattle is slowly dimmed in, and lights on* PASTOR *are slowly dimmed out*) . . . and grant such seasonable weather that we may yet be saved, that we may yet reap the fruits of our labors in the fields, and rejoice in thy goodness.

VOICES FROM CONGREGATION: Amen!

(*Picture projection is fully up, and light on* PASTOR *is completely out.*)

VOICE OF LIVING NEWSPAPER (*over* LOUDSPEAKER): The sun bakes the soil. Dust covers the land. All green things wither. Cattle die for lack of food and water.

Close Portals

SCENE EIGHTEEN
(*Wheat Pit*)

CHARACTERS

GROUP OF THIRTY TRADERS
VOICE OVER LOUDSPEAKER
RUNNERS
MEN AT TELEPHONE
CLERK AT BLACKBOARD

(*At rise:* TRADERS *are discovered in new formalized grouping, to indicate a different set-up from that of the first Wheat Pit scene. Volume and tempo pick up at level and speed at which first Wheat Pit scene blacked out. Gong rings,* LOUDSPEAKER *announces: "Fair and warmer."*

This time quotations are read in unison by everyone, and all their actions are in unison. The thermometer rises to indicate increasing heat, the dial on the clock moves over the specific areas indicating the hot summer months.)

TRADER NUMBER ONE: $1.01.*

VOICE (*over* LOUDSPEAKER): Fair and warmer, fair and warmer, fair and warmer.

TRADER NUMBER TWO: $1.02.

TRADER NUMBER THREE: $1.03.

TRADER NUMBER FOUR: $1.04.

TRADER NUMBER FIVE: $1.05.

TRADER NUMBER SIX: $1.06.

TRADER NUMBER SEVEN: $1.07.

TRADER NUMBER EIGHT: $1.08.

TRADER NUMBER NINE: $1.09.

TRADER NUMBER TEN: $1.10.

TRADER NUMBER ELEVEN: $1.11.

TRADER NUMBER TWELVE: $1.12.

Blackout

SCENE NINETEEN
(*Cotton Patch*) †

CHARACTERS

SAM, A NEGRO FARMER

THE SHERIFF

(*The scene is done with lights, the action suggesting that the locale is a Negro's tiny patch of cotton in the South.*

* Prices at height of drought, *New York Times*, August 1, 1934, *et supra; Journal of Commerce*, August 1, 1934, *et supra.*
† Creative.

The action also indicates the presence of a mule. As the lights come up SAM *is trudging slowly towards left and singing.)*

SAM (*singing*):

> Sho' 'nuff got a mule.
> Sho' 'nuff have.
> Sho' 'nuff goin' raise a crop
> Sho' 'nuff am.

(*He stops singing and begins to admire his mule*) Boy! Yo' sho' is a purty mule. Ol' Guv'ment goin' to be mighty pleased with yo'! Yeah, man! Yo' sho' look like you goin' pull dis ol' patch back.

(*The* SHERIFF *enters silently and stands behind* SAM.)

SAM (*continuing*): Long time since I drive a purty mule like yo'. I'se goin' call you Guv'ment. Yeah, man! Dey's whe' yo' come from an' dat's what I call yo'. Ol' Guv'ment say, "Sam, yo' take dis money and buy yo'self a plah an' a mule an' raise yo' a crop."

SHERIFF (*stepping forward*): That is a pretty mule, Sam.

SAM: Oh, howdy, Mr. Sheriff. I didn't know yo' was there.

SHERIFF: Where did you get that mule, Sam?

SAM: I got me a farm loan. The Guv'ment man down to Raleigh, he give it an' he say: "Yo' go 'head raise yo'self a money crop, but don't plant cotton."

SHERIFF: Sam, you still owe taxes on this place.

SAM: How much taxes I owed, Mr. Sheriff? I'm goin' have me a crop this year.

SHERIFF: What's the difference what you owe, Sam, you ain't agoin' to pay it. I gotta take this mule.

SAM (*alarmed*): Mr. Sheriff, yo' ain't goin' take my mule, is you?

SHERIFF: Sure am.

SAM: Doggone! Yo' tuk ma' other mule.

SHERIFF: Gotta have taxes. (*Walks toward mule*) Come on, mule, we gotta get goin'. (*To* SAM) What you call this mule to make him go?

SAM (*woefully*): I calls him Guv'ment.

SHERIFF: Giddap, Guv'ment!

Blackout

SCENE TWENTY
(*Sharecroppers*)

CHARACTERS

VOICE OF LIVING NEWSPAPER
FIRST SHARECROPPER
SECOND SHARECROPPER
THIRD SHARECROPPER
FOURTH SHARECROPPER
FIFTH SHARECROPPER

VOICE OF LIVING NEWSPAPER (*over* LOUDSPEAKER): It is estimated three hundred and seventy-five thousand sharecroppers lose their places in acreage reduction.*
(*It is possible that a scene column might be used to indicate the veranda of a Southern plantation. Five* SHARECROPPERS *enter, all very shabbily dressed.*)

FARMER (*drawling*): I guess I can't use you croppers no more. Ain't raisin' no more cotton.

FIRST CROPPER: I heard tell you got money for not raisin' cotton.

SECOND CROPPER: We figgered some of that was ours.

FARMER: Since when you croppers started figgerin'? You git

---

* Estimated figure—H. L. Mitchell, Executive Secretary, based on letter from Southern Tenant Farmers' Union, Memphis, Tenn.

you' stuff together and git. The Guv'ment ain't wantin'
me to plant the land you been workin'.

THIRD CROPPER: Wait a minute. The Guv'ment's payin' you
not to plant, and it says here . . . (*Waves a paper*)
. . . that you're supposed to pay us.

FARMER: Every durn one of you owes me money, and I ain't
a-sayin' nothin' if you git.

THIRD CROPPER: C'mon, croppers. I want to talk to you
alone. (*He draws them away from the* FARMER *who stands
watching them suspiciously*) Listen. (*The others crowd
around him*) The way I figger it, this Guv'ment stuff may
be a-helpin' us. Them Congressmen said we wouldn't lose
our homes, but, by God, we *are* losin' our homes. I ain't
been wantin' to join the Union 'cause I was afeared. But,
by God, I ain't afeared no more! The Union is demandin' ten cents an hour for cotton pickers. It's demandin'
Constitutional rights. I don't know how it's agoin' to get
'em. But, by God, I'm a'goin' to help 'em. Are you with
me? Then, come on! (*They follow him toward the*
FARMER *as the scene blackens.*)

Blackout

SCENE TWENTY-ONE
(*Meat Strike*)

CHARACTERS

VOICE OF LIVING NEWSPAPER

MAN

WOMAN

GROUP OF WOMEN WITH BANNERS

FEW MEN IN THE SAME GROUP

MAN LEAVING BUTCHER SHOP

VOICE OF LIVING NEWSPAPER (*over* LOUDSPEAKER): Detroit, July 27th, 1935. Housewives rebel against high meat prices.*

(*Butcher shop window and door. Meat prices displayed in window as follows:* †

ROUND STEAK	35¢ lb.
BEEF POT ROAST	21¢ lb.
VEAL ROAST	27¢ lb.
LEG OF LAMB	27¢ lb.
LOIN	29¢ lb.
HAM	31¢ lb.

Then lights come up on TWO WOMEN *carrying the following banners:* "WOMAN'S ACTION COMMITTEE—AGAINST HIGH COST OF LIVING." "ALL OUT TO PICKET FRIDAY AND SATURDAY." "STRIKE FOR A 20 PER CENT CUT IN MEAT PRICES." *They cross stage right to left. A* MAN *and* WOMAN *start crossing from left. As they come to entrance of store, they start to enter.* WOMAN *notices the picketing, and pulls* MAN *away from doorway.*)

WOMAN: Don't go in there! There's a strike. We'll go some other place to buy!

(*They start walking to right. Suddenly a* MAN *comes through the door with a package. A number of* WOMEN *come on from left. They see the* MAN, *and start for him.*)

GROUP OF WOMEN (*ad lib.*): Don't let him pass! Get him! Strikebreaker. The package! Get the package. Show him we mean business. Get him!

(*As the* MAN *emerges from the mob, his package is seized by a woman who rips it apart and throws it off stage. He is then surrounded by a furious mob intent upon tearing him to pieces. The* FEMALE LEADER *of the strike mounts a box.*)

* *New York Times,* July 28, 1935.
† *Ibid.,* August 6, 1935.

42 TRIPLE-A PLOWED UNDER

LEADER: Wait! We've got a bigger fight than this on our hands. We're not going to be satisfied with boycotting only butcher shops. Once organized we'll look into milk prices, and gas and electricity rates. In the present strike we don't want the small butchers to suffer. We want to get results from the big packing houses!

MALE VOICE: Why don't you go to Washington? They started this.

LEADER: Maybe they started it by killing the little pigs and cattle. We don't know and we don't care. But we're not going to pay such high prices for meat, and that's all there is to it!

VOICES: We won't buy meat. Prices must come down. We won't buy meat! Prices must come down. (*The roar of a truck coming to a stop is heard off stage.*)

LEADER: A meat truck! A packing-house truck. Soak the meat in kerosene!

VOICES (*ad lib.*): Kerosene on the meat. Soak the meat. Down with the meat packer millionaires. Prices must come down. We won't buy! We won't buy! We won't buy! We won't buy!

(MOB *rushes off. They all exit down left.*)

Blackout

SCENE TWENTY-TWO
(*Mrs. Dorothy Sherwood*)

CHARACTERS

VOICE OF LIVING NEWSPAPER
POLICE LIEUTENANT
MRS. DOROTHY SHERWOOD
POLICEMAN
OFF STAGE VOICES ON MICROPHONE

VOICE OF LIVING NEWSPAPER (*over* LOUDSPEAKER): Newburgh, New York: August 20th, 1935. Mrs. Dorothy Sherwood.* (*Police desk on right. Light on desk, with* POLICE LIEUTENANT *behind it. Enter* MRS. SHERWOOD, *left, with dead infant in her arms. She walks toward desk.*)

MRS. SHERWOOD: He's dead. I drowned him.

LIEUTENANT: You what?

MRS. SHERWOOD: I just drowned my son. I couldn't feed him, and I couldn't bear to see him hungry. . . . I let him wade in the creek until he got tired. Then I led him out into the middle, and held him there until he stopped moving.

LIEUTENANT (*calling, not loudly*): John! (POLICEMAN *approaches*) Take the body. Book this woman for murder. (POLICEMAN *takes child from her.*)

(*Blackout on everything except* MRS. SHERWOOD. *She is picked out by the solitary overhead light. Off stage* VOICE *comes through the* LOUDSPEAKER.)

VOICE: Why did you do it?

MRS. SHERWOOD: I couldn't feed him. I had only five cents.

VOICE: Your own child. Did you think you were doing the right thing?

MRS. SHERWOOD: I just thought it had to be done, that's all. It was the best thing to do.

VOICE: How could a mother kill her own child?

MRS. SHERWOOD: He was hungry, I tell you. Hungry, hungry, hungry, hungry, *hungry!* (*As her voice mounts it is blended with that of another which commences a progression of nine voices crying "Guilty!" These come over the* LOUDSPEAKER *and are varied in color, but increasing in fervor until—*

Dim-out

* *Daily News,* August 21, 1935.

SCENE TWENTY-THREE
(Supreme Court . . . AAA killed)

CHARACTERS

VOICE OF LIVING NEWSPAPER
VOICE OVER LOUDSPEAKER
SUPREME COURT JUSTICE ROBERTS—figure in silhouette
SUPREME COURT JUSTICE STONE—figure in silhouette
SEVEN OTHER SUPREME COURT JUSTICES—figures in silhouette
DANIEL O. HASTINGS, SENATOR FROM DELAWARE—in silhouette
ALFRED E. SMITH—in silhouette
EARL BROWDER—in silhouette
THOMAS JEFFERSON—in silhouette
FIRST MAN
SECOND MAN
THIRD MAN
A WOMAN
FOURTH MAN
FIFTH MAN

VOICE OF LIVING NEWSPAPER (*over* LOUDSPEAKER): January 6, 1936. . . . Supreme Court invalidates AAA in Hoosac Mills case.*

VOICE (*also over* LOUDSPEAKER): The majority opinion—Justice Roberts.

(As travelers open from rear, projection of Constitution is thrown on glass curtain. Discovered in shadow against projection are JUSTICE STONE, THREE OTHER JUSTICES, *then* JUSTICE ROBERTS, *and the* FOUR REMAINING JUSTICES, *right.* ROBERTS *rises to one-foot platform directly in front of him.* FIVE JUSTICES *who concurred in his opinion, turn in profile as he begins to speak.)*

* *New York Times*, January 7, 1936.

JUSTICE ROBERTS: . . . Beyond cavil the sole objective of the legislation is to restore the purchasing price of agricultural products to a parity with that prevailing in an earlier day; to take money from the processor and bestow it on the farmers. The Constitution is the supreme law of the land, ordained and established by the people. All legislation must conform to the principles it lays down. The power to confer or withhold unlimited benefits is the power to coerce or destroy. This is coercion by economic pressure. The judgment is affirmed.*

(*He steps down;* JUSTICE STONE *steps up.*)

VOICE OVER LOUDSPEAKER: The minority opinion—Justice Stone.

(*The* FIVE JUSTICES *concurring with* JUSTICE ROBERTS *turn to full front. The* TWO *concurring with* STONE, *turn in silhouette.*)

JUSTICE STONE: Courts are concerned with the power to enact statutes, not with their wisdom. The only check upon their own exercise of power is our own sense of self-restraint. For the removal of unwise laws from the statute books, appeal lies not to the courts, but to the ballot, and to the processes of democratic government.

So may the judicial power be abused. "The power to tax is the power to destroy," but we do not for that reason doubt its existence. Courts are not the only agents of government which must be assumed to have the capacity to govern.†

(*As* JUSTICE STONE *steps down,* SENATOR HASTINGS *enters, right, steps on higher platform at back, throwing his shadow into a much larger projection than that of the* JUSTICES.)

SENATOR HASTINGS: This re-establishes Constitutional government. It gives back to the States the power they in-

* *New York Times,* January 7, 1936.
† *Ibid.*

tended to reserve when they adopted the Constitution.
The chances are it will improve the condition of the
country, as did the decision of the NRA.*

(HASTINGS *steps down and exits left.* ALFRED E. SMITH
enters right, steps on platform vacated by HASTINGS.)

ALFRED E. SMITH: We don't want the Congress of the United
States singly or severally to tell the Supreme Court what
to do. We don't want any administration that takes a
shot at the Constitution in the dark, and tries to put
something over in contradiction of it, upon any theory
that there is going to be a great public power in favor
of it, and it is possible that the United States Supreme
Court may be intimidated into a friendly opinion with
respect to it. But I found, all during my public life, that
Almighty God built this country, and he did not give us
that kind of a Supreme Court.†

(SMITH *steps down, and exits left.* BROWDER *enters right;
steps on platform vacated by* SMITH.)

EARL BROWDER: The reactionaries seek to turn both "Amer-
icanism" and the Constitution into instruments of reaction, but neither of these things belongs to them. No-
where does the Constitution grant the Supreme Court
power over Congress, but it does make Congress the
potential master of the Supreme Court.‡ I repeat, the
Constitution of the United States does not give the Supreme Court the right to declare laws passed by Congress unconstitutional.§

(BROWDER *steps down and exits left.* THOMAS JEFFERSON
enters right, steps on platform vacated by BROWDER.)

THOMAS JEFFERSON: There must be an arbiter somewhere.
True, there must. But does that prove it is either the
Congress or the Supreme Court? The ultimate arbiter

* *New York Times,* January 7, 1936.
† *Ibid.,* January 26, 1936.
‡ *Daily Worker,* February 13, 1936.
§ *Ibid.,* January 11, 1936.

is the people of the Union, assembled by their deputies in convention at the call of Congress or two-thirds of the States.*

(*Travelers slowly close, with* JEFFERSON *remaining standing on platform, center.*)

VOICE OVER LOUDSPEAKER: Farmers voted, by more than 6 to 1, for continuance of Triple-A.† (MEN *start crossing stage in front of travelers, from right to left.*)

FIRST MAN: The AAA is dead. . . . (*Exits left.*)

SECOND MAN: No more allotment checks. . . . (*Exits left.*)

THIRD MAN: What the hell're we agoin' to do this winter? (*Exits left.*)

A WOMAN: How're we goin' t' get coal? (*Exits left.*)

FOURTH MAN: They say the people wrote the Constitution. . . . (*Exits left.*)

FIFTH MAN: Them people have been dead a long time. . . . (*Also exits.*)

Blackout

<h2 align="center">SCENE TWENTY-FOUR</h2>
(The Big "Steal")

<h3 align="center">CHARACTERS</h3>

VOICE OF LIVING NEWSPAPER
HENRY A. WALLACE, SECRETARY OF AGRICULTURE

VOICE OF LIVING NEWSPAPER (*over* LOUDSPEAKER): January 21st, Buffalo, New York, Court refunds processing tax on order of Supreme tribunal.‡ (*Pause*) Secretary Wallace. (*Lights on* WALLACE *speaking into microphone.*)

---

* Jefferson's letter to Mr. Johnson, June 12, 1823—in *Congressional Digest*, December, 1935.

† *World Almanac*, 1936, p. 167.

‡ *New York Times*, January 21, 1936.

SECRETARY WALLACE: . . . It doesn't make sense. In the Hoosac Mills case the Supreme Court disapproved the idea that the Government could take money from one group for the benefit of another. Yet in turning over to the processors this $200,000,000 which came from all the people, we are seeing the most flagrant example of expropriation for the benefit of one small group. You will get some idea of its size when you contrast these refunds with the profits of the processors in their most prosperous years. Cotton mills reported profits of $30,-000,000 in 1920. Their processing tax refunds amount to $51,000,000 in cotton. Flour mills reported profits of about $20,000,000 on their wheat flour business in 1929. Their processing tax refunds amount to $67,000,000. Packers' profits on their hog business in 1929 were in the neighborhood of $20,000,000. Their tax refunds were $51,000,000.

This return of the processing tax under order of the Supreme Court is probably the greatest legalized steal in American history! *

Blackout

SCENE TWENTY-FIVE
(*Soil Conservation*)

CHARACTERS

VOICE OF LIVING NEWSPAPER
CHESTER A. DAVIS—Administrator of AAA
FIRST REPORTER
SECOND REPORTER
MESSENGER
CLERKS, STENOGRAPHERS, ETC.

* *New York Times,* January 29, 1936.

VOICE OF LIVING NEWSPAPER (*over* LOUDSPEAKER): Washington, January 1936. Administrator Chester A. Davis.*
(*Light upon* CHESTER A. DAVIS; *this scene is played around his desk.*)

CHESTER A. DAVIS: . . . and we've got to find something to take the place of AAA . . . something that is constitutional, and that the various farm blocs will approve. . . .

FIRST REPORTER (*slowly after a slight pause*): Why don't you use the Soil Conservation Act passed last year? Sure, that's the one.

SECOND REPORTER: It's as broad as Barnum and Bailey's tent and it covers all the ground the AAA did.

CHESTER A. DAVIS (*scornfully*): Impossible. That Act was just a temporary stop-gap dealing with the WPA or something. It has no bearing on this case.

FIRST REPORTER: I tell you it has. I was looking it over this morning and . . .

SECOND REPORTER (*excitedly*): I was with him. It authorized conservation, acquisition of land, compensation for farmers who . . .

CHESTER A. DAVIS (*holding up his hand*): Wait a minute. (*He presses a button on his desk and speaks into the telephone*) Send in some copies of the Soil Conservation Act. (*There is an expectant silence as they regard each other. The* REPORTERS *are excited,* DAVIS *smiles skeptically. A* MESSENGER *enters and deposits some sheaves of paper on his desk.* DAVIS *takes one, and the* REPORTERS *make a dash for the others. As* DAVIS *reads, the* OTHERS *read along with him. When they break into speech, it is in tones of intense excitement.* CHESTER DAVIS *speaks up, reading*) The Soil Conservation Act passed on mmm (*mumbling*) . . . and authorized the creation of mm-mm-mm-mm-mm-mm-mm. *One:*—Conservation measures including

* Scene based on article in *Time Magazine,* January 27, 1936.

methods of cultivation, the growing of vegetation and changes in the use of land. . . . *Two:*—Co-operation of agreements with any agency or any person. . . . *Three:*— Acquisition of lands or rights or interest therein. . . .

SECOND REPORTER (*excitedly*): *Four:* United States Government contributions to those who conserve the soil, *in form of money, services, materials, or otherwise.*

FIRST REPORTER: *Five:* The hiring of employees.

SECOND REPORTER (*more excited than he was before*): *Six:* The expenditure of money for *anything,* from the purchasing of law books right down to passenger-carrying vehicles. (*The words rushing out*) And most important of all . . .

Seven: the transfer to this work authorized of such functions, moneys, personnel, and the property of other agencies in the Department of Agriculture as the Secretary may see fit!

CHESTER DAVIS (*who has become progressively more excited though inarticulate to this point—jumping up*): My God, there's the farm program for 1936. (*Tremendous excitement, elation, his fingers begin to punch the various buttons on his desk, sending out a general alarm. Simultaneously,* SECRETARIES, ASSISTANTS, STENOGRAPHERS, CLERKS *rush in. He continues, shouting*): Get my Planning Board together. Get my assistant, get me Wallace. Get me Wilson, get me Stedman, get me . . . (SECRETARIES, CLERKS, MESSENGERS *cross and crisscross from right to left as* DAVIS *gives orders.*)

Blackout

SCENE TWENTY-SIX
(Finale)

CHARACTERS

VOICE OF LIVING NEWSPAPER
DELEGATION OF FARMERS CARRYING PLACARDS, REPRESENTING:
  South Dakota
  Minnesota
  North Dakota
  Wisconsin
  Nebraska
  Iowa
  Kansas
  Idaho
  Indiana

SECRETARY WALLACE
MAN IN EVENING CLOTHES   } from Scene Fifteen
WOMAN IN EVENING CLOTHES

WOMAN STRIKE LEADER   } from Scene Twenty
OTHER WOMAN

FARMER
DEALER   } from Scene Three
MANUFACTURER

WORKER
A GROUP OF UNEMPLOYED WORKERS
A GROUP OF UNEMPLOYED FARMERS

VOICE OF LIVING NEWSPAPER: Huron, South Dakota, February 20th, 1936. . . . Farmers meet in Convention to draft program.*

* *Farmers' National Weekly,* February 14, 1936.

(Portals part just sufficiently to admit line of FARMERS *carrying banners of the States—South Dakota, Minnesota, North Dakota, Wisconsin, Nebraska, Iowa, Kansas, Idaho and Indiana. Half of the* FARMERS *enter from the left, and go right in front of portals, the other half enter from right and go left in front of portals. As last* FARMER *enters, portals close and straight line evenly spaced is formed in front of portals.)*

VOICE (*over* LOUDSPEAKER): Now, while the Soil Conservation Act is being written, is the time to make Congress and the Administration feel the pressure of the organized good sense of the American farmers. We believe that the following main points represent what the farmers must have in order to live decently, and at the same time protect the interests of the other sections of the working population.*

FARMER FROM SOUTH DAKOTA: Past commitments for the benefit payments under the old AAA must be paid in full.

FARMER FROM MINNESOTA: Whatever legislation may be passed should include cash payments to working farmers *at least equal* to the benefit payments under the AAA.

FARMER FROM NORTH DAKOTA (*one step forward*): Additional cash relief if the benefit payments are inadequate for a farm family to maintain a decent American standard of living.

FARMER FROM WISCONSIN: A decent American standard of living means cost of production prices.

FARMER FROM NEBRASKA: Cost of production prices mean far higher prices than today, whereby the farmer can at least pay his bills, operating costs and living expenses.

FARMER FROM IOWA: Increased production is needed by the

* *Farmers' National Weekly,* February 7, 1936.

nation today, the United States Department of Agriculture reports.

VOICE (*over* LOUDSPEAKER): To feed one hundred and twenty-five million people according to the best standards, forty million acres would have to be added to production.

FARMER FROM KANSAS: Therefore we oppose the policy of reduction . . .

FARMER FROM IDAHO: . . . but we do not oppose soil conservation except when used as a means of giving the Secretary of Agriculture power to force farmers to reduce production of good land.

FARMER FROM INDIANA: There are adequate resources available to meet the financial obligation incurred in this program. We suggest diversion to farm relief of a large part of the immense war appropriations, and increasing taxation on the wealth and income of the great financial and industrial interests of this country. *With special emphasis on the giant corporations which handle food productions!*

FARMER FROM SOUTH DAKOTA: The farmer has been sold down the river.

(*Curtains part revealing full stage set.* MAN *and* WOMAN *in evening clothes are on highest level upstage left.* SECRETARY WALLACE *is on intermediate level upstage,* WOMEN *from the Meat Strike scene are left center in front of* WALLACE, *and* MAN *and* WOMAN *in evening clothes and* UNEMPLOYED *are on ramp, right, while* FARMERS *are on ramp, left.*

FARMERS *previously in line across footlights move toward ramp left, a few to proscenium, down right.* FARMER, UNEMPLOYED, *etc., when speaking, step a little forward so that they may be marked apart from crowd. All on stage turn heads toward speaker to indicate source of voice.*

The reaction is particularly marked in case of LOUD-
SPEAKER, *with all heads turned toward voice and holding
that position until* LOUDSPEAKER *is finished. Other defi-
nite and marked reactions in this scene are gestures on
the "up, up" of the* FARMERS, *and the "down, down"
of the* WOMEN; *the movement of* FARMERS *and* UNEM-
PLOYED *as the* FARMER *steps forward between the two
groups, and the gestures drawing them together on the
line, "then our problem is the same," gestures toward
and against* MAN *and* WOMAN *in evening clothes and*
SECRETARY WALLACE *on lines such as "no charity," "jobs,"
"jobs." "We need help, not words." There should be a
balanced reaction away from crowd in fear, disgust, etc.,
on the part of the* MAN *and* WOMAN *in evening clothes.*)

SECRETARY WALLACE: In 1935 the AAA paid benefits of five
hundred and eighty million dollars.*

A FARMER: † Soil Conservation benefits must at least be
equal to the benefits of the Triple-A.

MAN IN EVENING CLOTHES: We must carry on with soil conservation.

VOICE (*over* LOUDSPEAKER): A dollar one, a dollar two . . .

ANOTHER FARMER (*taking step forward*): Soil Conservation
is the Triple-A in false whiskers.

STILL ANOTHER FARMER: Farm prices must stay up.

WOMAN (*strike leader*): Food prices must go down.

ALL FARMERS (*in chorus*): UP! UP!

ALL WOMEN: DOWN! DOWN!

FARMER ‡ (*from Scene Three*): I can't buy that auto.

DEALER (*from Scene Three*): I can't take that shipment.

MANUFACTURER (*from Scene Three*): I can't use you any
more. (*Jumps to intermediate level.*)

---

* *New York Times,* March 4, 1936.
† Creative and digest of news.
‡ Digest of article "A.A.A. Philosophy" by Rexford G. Tugwell,
Fortune Magazine, January 1934.

WORKER (*from Scene Three*): I can't eat. (*Jumps to intermediate level.*)

VOICE (*over* LOUDSPEAKER): There is now piled up in the banks a huge savings reserve, and it lays a basis for a new speculative boom— (*All look toward* LOUDSPEAKER.)

MAN IN EVENING CLOTHES: * Back to normalcy.

VOICE (*over* LOUDSPEAKER): . . . which may result in a far more disastrous collapse than any heretofore experienced.

MAN IN EVENING CLOTHES (*to woman with him*): The rugged individualism of our forefathers will solve our problem.

A FARMER: Our problems are of the soil.

AN UNEMPLOYED WORKER: Ours of the belly.

MAN IN EVENING CLOTHES: Of course we need the farmer.

VOICE (*over* LOUDSPEAKER): A dollar three, a dollar four . . .

SECRETARY WALLACE: We have come to the time when we have to learn to live one with another. We have no more cheap land, no great foreign markets, no one to impose upon.

A FARMER: We need help, not words!

SECRETARY WALLACE: We, down in Washington, do not believe we have the final answer to the problem—but we believe that, no matter who is in power a year hence, the kind of thing exemplified in the Soil Conservation Act will be going forward.

ONE FARMER: We need help!

ALL FARMERS: We need help!

ONE UNEMPLOYED: We need food!

ALL UNEMPLOYED: We need food!

ALL FARMERS: We need food!

ONE WOMAN: We need a decent standard of living.

ALL WOMEN: We need a decent standard of living.

ALL UNEMPLOYED: So do we. We need a decent standard of living.

* Remainder of scene is creative.

ALL FARMERS: So do we.

A FARMER: Then all our problems are the same!

ALL UNEMPLOYED: Then all our problems are the same.

WOMAN IN EVENING CLOTHES: All must be helped, John.

FARMER, UNEMPLOYED AND WOMEN: No charity!

AN UNEMPLOYED: Jobs!

ALL UNEMPLOYED: Jobs!

A FARMER: Help.

AN UNEMPLOYED: We need a State that permits no man to go hungry.

MAN IN EVENING CLOTHES: Rugged individualism.

A WOMAN: No profiteering.

ALL UNEMPLOYED: Jobs.

ONE FARMER: We can't harvest.

ALL FARMERS: We can't harvest.

ONE WOMAN: We can't buy.

ALL WOMEN: We can't buy.

ONE UNEMPLOYED: We can't eat!

ALL UNEMPLOYED: We can't eat!

VOICE (*over* LOUDSPEAKER. *News flashes of events that have occurred that day—especially with reference to a Farmer-Labor Party. Below are three flashes that were used*): *

Local Farmer-Labor Party conventions in Connecticut, Massachusetts, Pennsylvania and South Dakota declared for a national Farmer-Labor Party. Two county conventions at Minneapolis passed a resolution demanding that the State Farmer-Labor Party meeting in convention at Minneapolis March 17th, take the lead in a national Farmer-Labor Party.

Washington: Before a cheering audience at the St. Nicholas Arena last night, Congressman Ernest Lundeen,

* Daily spot newspaper quotes used, quotes changing with the news.

of Minnesota, said: "Labor unions and farmer organizations will soon become irresistible political powers."

Great Falls, Montana: The semi-annual conference of the Farmers' Holiday Association held here today had as its major decision the endorsement of a resolution for the formation of a Farmer-Labor Party. This resolution was proposed by Reid Robinson of the Butte Miners' Union.

FARMER: We *need* you.
CHORUS OF FARMERS: We *need* you.
LEADER OF UNEMPLOYED: We need *you.*
CHORUS OF UNEMPLOYED: We need *you.* (FARMERS *and* UN-EMPLOYED *jump close together, arms extended. Light on them is intensified. Lights on* WALLACE *and* WOMAN *and* MAN *in evening clothes fade. Tableau of* FARMERS, WOMEN *and* UNEMPLOYED *hold.*)

Curtain

POWER

A Living Newspaper

SPONSORED BY
THE NEWSPAPER GUILD OF AMERICA

BY ARTHUR ARENT

THE SUPREME COURT HEARING ARGUMENTS ON THE TVA APPEAL

Federal Theatre Photo by Arthur Steiner

Power was first produced at the Ritz Theatre, New York City, on February 23, 1937, with the following cast:

ACT ONE

Voice of the Living Newspaper   Charles Dill

Opening

Electricians
          Robert Noack, Jack Denver, Seymour Malmude
Old Man at Radio   Charles Danforth
His Wife   Jean Thomas
Police Operator   Charles T. Lewis
Doctor   Gregory Robbins
Interne   Peter Marvin
Nurses   Eleanora Barrie, Ethel Jones, Lillian Shrewsbury
Policeman   James Swift
Irish Mother   Marjorie Betts
Traffic Accident Victim   Guerita Donnelly
Driver of Car   Muni Diamond
Airport Radio Operator   Burton Mallory
Theatre Manager   Joe Rose
Restaurant Proprietor   Boris Korlin
Bakery Proprietor   Frank McMunn

Inventors

Announcer   Jack Lorenz
William Gilbert (1600)   Wilfred Clark
Michael Faraday (1821)   H. H. McCollum
Georg Simon Ohm (1826)   Harry Brooks
Zenobe T. Gramme (1873)   Allan Tower

3

P O W E R

Thomas A. Edison (1879)   Dudley Hawley

Business Men

     Bernard Pate, Maurice MacNevin, Robert Noack, Burton Mallory, Charles T. Lewis, Warren Pittenger

Financier   William Roselle

Kilowatt Hour

Consumer   Norman Lloyd

Electrician   Robert Noack

Grocery Clerks   Boris Korlin, Joe Rose

Butchers   Joseph Murray, Kermit Augustine

Electric Company Manager   Allan Tower

Expansion

T. Commerford Martin   William Roselle

Park Bench—1907

Man on Bench   Wilfred Clark

Policeman   Frank McMunn

Fair Profits

Consumer   Norman Lloyd

Chairman   James F. Kelly

Directors   Harry Brooks, H. H. McCollum

Witness   Bernard Pate

Commissioners   Dudley Hawley, Edward LeDuc

Harlow S. Persons   Ulric Collins

Holding Company

Man Who Knows   Robert Noack

Stage Hands

     Charles T. Lewis, James Swift, Joseph Murray, Richard Keller

Martin Insull   Charles Danforth

Senator George W. Norris   Burton Mallory

Senator Sherman Minton   James F. Kelly

Senator Burton K. Wheeler — Dudley Hawley
The Messrs. Carmichael — Bernard Pate
Consumer Angus T. Buttonkooper — Norman Lloyd

Childish Questions

Father — Allan Tower
Daughter — Viola Swayne

Insull's Empire

Samuel J. Insull — H. H. McCollum
Consumer-Investor — Norman Lloyd

Cost Comparison (1913-1926)

Mr. Lane — Bernard Pate
Mrs. Lane of 1913 — Eleanora Barrie
Mrs. Lane of 1926 — Warda Howard
Fruit Vendors — Boris Korlin, Richard Keller
Hardware Clerks — Edward LeDuc, Maurice MacNevin
Drygoods Clerks — Muni Diamond, Seymour Malmude
Rent Collectors — Robert Noack, Peter Marvin
Electric Company Clerks — Warren Pittenger, James Swift

Consumer Sues

Consumer — Norman Lloyd

Propaganda

Editor — Harry Brooks
Utilities Representative — Dudley Hawley
J. L. Murphy — William Roselle
Robert E. Healy — Gregory Robbins
Willard Cope — Dudley Hawley
M. H. Aylesworth — Charles Danforth
College Professors
Frank McMunn, Joseph Murray, Charles Deighan, James F. Kelly, Boris Korlin, Allan Tower
Senator George W. Norris — Burton Mallory

"Get Norris"

Grocer   Charles T. Lewis
Politician   William Roselle

Municipal Ownership

Mayor Clare W. H. Bangs   Edward LeDuc
His Secretary   James Swift
Carl D. Thompson   Allan Tower
Federal Trade Commission Spokesman   Gregory Robbins
Bernard F. Weadock   James F. Kelly
Representative John E. Rankin   Ulric Collins
Second Congressman   Robert Mack
Third Congressman   Joseph Barrett

The Tennessee Valley

Farmer   Wilfred Clark
Farmer's Wife   Jean Thomas
City Dweller   John Lorenz
His Wife   Guerita Donnelly
Electric Company Manager   Frank McMunn
Public Utilities Commissioner   Harry Brooks
Clerk of Senate   Charles Danforth

ACT TWO

Small-Town Meeting

Chairman   Edward LeDuc
Barber   Joe Rose
Grocer   James Swift
Butcher   Charles T. Lewis
Storekeeper   William Perloff

Farmers' Meeting

Chairman   Ulric Collins
Farmers

Frank Burke, Jack Sheppard, Robert Mack, William
LaVar, Joseph Barrett, Sandy Ackline, John Donahue

Directors' Meeting

Chairman   James F. Kelly
Directors
    Dudley Hawley, Allan Tower, Bernard Pate, Harry
    Brooks, Frank McMunn, H. H. McCollum

Competition

Farmer   Wilfred Clark
Linesmen   Richard Keller, Robert Noack
Old Woman   Edith Harcourt
Voice of Linesman   James Swift
Colored Farmer   Milton Williams
Company Agents   Warren Pittenger, Gregory Robbins
Catoosa County (Ga.) Residents
    Charles T. Lewis, Muni Diamond, Alonzo McWaith,
    Peter Marvin, Kermit Augustine

1934 Coffin Award

Wendell L. Willkie   William Roselle
Frank W. Smith   Allan Tower

Finale

Voice of Chief Justice Hughes   Dudley Hawley
Voice of Justice McReynolds   James F. Kelly
Forney Johnston   Bernard Pate
James M. Beck   H. H. McCollum
John Lord O'Brian   Charles Danforth
Farmer   Wilfred Clark
Business Man   H. H. McCollum
City Man   Jack Lorenz
Consumer-at-Large   Warren Pittenger
Governor Bibb Graves   Allan Tower
Governor Hill McAlister   Edward LeDuc
Senator George W. Norris   Burton Mallory
James Lawrence Fly   Charles Danforth

8   P O W E R

Representative John E. Rankin   Ulric Collins
Marchers, Consumers, Housewives, etc.

    Kate Cloud, Mary L. Burrill, Agnes Moss, Florence Knight, Frances Ware, Elizabeth Bilencova, Kay Powers, Marie Edwards, Peggy Bird, Ivan Acharg, Emily Stern, John H. Lee, Louise Bail, Alex Ackland, Samuel Raskyn, Virginia Drew, Laura Strassman, Benjamin Wallace, Mae Hendricks, Amelia Barleon, Harriet Capaldo, Charles Bloomfield, John Hawkins, Jack Shipman, Eva Connell, Elsie Earle, Sala Staw, Joseph Rivers

Directed by Brett Warren

Stage Designs by Howard Bay

Music by Lee Wainer

Costume Designs by Kathryn Wilson

Technical Direction by Monroe B. Hack

Production Under the Supervision of Morris Watson

Living Newspaper Theatre Orchestra Conducted by Myron Roman, Federal Music Project

ACT ONE

SCENE ONE
(*Opening*)

CHARACTERS

VOICE OF LIVING NEWSPAPER

STAGE MANAGER

TWO ELECTRICIANS } At theatre switchboard

GIRLS, working at power machines

OLD MAN AT RADIO

OLD WOMAN } Listening to radio

POLICE RADIO OPERATOR at a microphone

DOCTOR

THREE NURSES } Around an operating table

ELECTRICIAN

FIRST POLICEMAN

SECOND POLICEMAN

OLD MAN

THEATRE MANAGER

IRISH MOTHER

BAKERY PROPRIETOR

AIRPORT RADIO OPERATOR

RESTAURANT PROPRIETOR

TRAFFIC ACCIDENT VICTIM

DRIVER OF CAR

VARIOUS MEN AND WOMEN

Following the overture, projection appears on the front curtain—"The Living Newspaper presents POWER." The word "Power" grows larger, the other words fade out.

9

The curtain rises quickly. The lights come up on two ELECTRICIANS *and a* STAGE MANAGER *at a portable switchboard. The* ELECTRICIANS *have hands on switches and their eyes on the* STAGE MANAGER.

LOUDSPEAKER: This is the switchboard of the Ritz Theatre. Through this board flows the electric power that amplifies my voice, the power that ventilates the theatre, and the power that lights this show.

STAGE MANAGER (*picking up a fat cable*): It all comes through here.

LOUDSPEAKER: Give us a demonstration of *Power!*

STAGE MANAGER: Sure, Charlie, take your X-Rays down to the mark and come up slowly on number three spot.

(*The* ELECTRICIANS *throw their switches, lights dim down on them, and come up on* GIRLS *working over electric sewing machines in a clothing factory.*)

LOUDSPEAKER: There are 4,000 clothing factories in the metropolitan area employing 115,000 persons.*

(*The machines hum with increasing volume and the* GIRLS *work with increasing speed. The hum turns to waltz music from* LOUDSPEAKER *as the lights dim down and come up on an* OLD MAN *and an* OLD WOMAN *sitting at a radio. Over the radio is heard "The Blue Danube Waltz."*)

LOUDSPEAKER: . . . Power! World communication! The world in your own home. . . . What would you do without your radio, Pop?

OLD MAN (*he hasn't heard*): Uh?

LOUDSPEAKER: Never mind. . . . Don't bother!

(*The lights dim down on the* OLD MAN *and* WOMAN. *Music over radio stops, as lights pick up* POLICE RADIO OPERATOR.)

* Labor Research Association, 1935 Census of Clothing Manfacturers.

POLICE RADIO OPERATOR: Calling cars forty-two and eight. Calling cars forty-two and eight. Proceed at once to 331 Belmont Avenue, 331 Belmont Avenue. . . . Hold-up! (*Continues ad libbing on "calling cars," etc., until his voice is drowned out by off-stage sound of sirens, and lights dim out.*)

LOUDSPEAKER: Call police headquarters and one of these radio patrol cars will be at your home in three minutes.* (*Lights come up on hospital group, nurses and doctors standing over form on operating table. One* NURSE *is sterilizing instruments.*)

LOUDSPEAKER: Oh, Doctor, I believe those electrically sterilized instruments are ready.

(*They continue to get ready for the operation.*)

LOUDSPEAKER: Electric power has revolutionized modern surgery. The number of lives saved in recent years through the invention and development of electrical equipment is incalculable.

(*Huge overhead drop-light lights up over the operation scene, as other lights in that area dim out. Suddenly a shrill police whistle is heard, the overhead light goes out on the hospital scene, and a red traffic light comes on. Again the shrill whistle is heard, and the light changes to green.*)

LOUDSPEAKER: Eighty-six hundred of these sentinels in New York City keep us from crashing our autos together, night and day. . . .† (*The traffic light flashes red and green rapidly, each change accompanied by a blast of the whistle*) . . . you flick lights on in your home with Power. . . . You heat your iron with Power. You clean with Power. . . . (*Lights come up on the various groups previously lit—the* POLICE RADIO OPERATOR, *hospital, factory and* OLD COUPLE *listening to the radio.* LOUD-

* New York City Police Radio Department.
† Chief Engineer's Office, New York Police Department.

SPEAKER *continues*) . . . You curl your hair, you cook, you even shave, all with Power! (*A loud detonation is heard off stage.*)

Blackout

LOUDSPEAKER (*excitedly—in the dark*): Flash: December 28th, 1936: Newark, New Jersey, and its suburbs were thrown into total darkness tonight when fire in a power plant cut off all electric current. Nearly a million people were affected.*

DOCTOR'S VOICE (*comes out of the darkness*): Flashlights, quick.

(NURSE *comes running with two flashes. One is passed to another* NURSE, *and they both flash lights over the* DOCTOR'S *shoulder as he goes on with the operation. His assistant lights up with a third flash. They hold for a second, and all three flashlights go out. All characters in remainder of this scene light their own faces for the duration of their speeches, either with telephones having small flashlights in the mouthpieces, or with pocket flashes.*)

ELECTRICIAN (*into telephone flashlight*): Operator, operator, get me Public Service. The power's off.

FIRST POLICEMAN (*at transmitter*): Calling all cars . . . calling all cars . . . calling all cars.

SECOND POLICEMAN (*running on*): Callahan, the lights are out. The entire city's dark.

FIRST POLICEMAN (*into telephone flashlight*): Hello, Brady! Notify all radio cars you can find to proceed to Public Service on the Kearny Meadows. All radio patrols phone in every two minutes. All leaves rescinded. I want every man on the job. (*Sound of police siren is heard over* LOUDSPEAKER.)

* *New York World-Telegram*, December 28, 1936.

OLD MAN (*into telephone flashlight*): Operator, operator, operator. . . .

BAKERY PROPRIETOR (*greatly agitated*): Operator, operator, my electric conveyor is stopped with four thousand dollars' worth of rolls in the oven! They're burning up! Four thousand dollars' worth! *

IRISH MOTHER (*Irish accent*): Operator, operator, the heater's off. My baby's got the flu.

THEATRE MANAGER (*Jewish dialect*): Operator, operator! By me the theatre is dark. Somebody blowed the fuse—the fuse. Two thousand people want the money back.†
(*Groans.*)

AIRPORT RADIO OPERATOR: This is the traffic control tower. Light your ground flares and smoke bombs. Call Floyd Bennett Field. Tell them to keep on their floodlights for emergency landings. There's a plane waiting to land and two more due in five minutes.‡

RESTAURANT PROPRIETOR (*Italian dialect, face lit by the fire of a match which he holds*): I wanta de lights—I wanta de lights. . . . Get the superintendent, I gotta no lights. . . . (*A police whistle is heard, then grinding of brakes followed by a crash. A woman screams. Slight pause, then:*)

VOICE—DRIVER OF CAR: My God, I didn't see her, I tell you, it was dark. . . . I didn't see her.
(*The following characters speak from different levels on the stage. Their faces are lit up by flashes which they put out immediately after speaking. This gives a zigzag lighting effect. Front traveler curtain starts to close.*)

MAN: Operator, operator, light. . . .

WOMAN: Operator, operator, light. . . .

MAN: Lights, lights. . . .

* *Newark Ledger,* December 29, 1936.
† *Newark Ledger,* December 29, 1936.
‡ Based on A.P. dispatch, *N. Y. World-Telegram,* December 29, 1936.

WOMAN: Lights, lights. . . .

MAN: Operator, operator. . . .

MAN: Operator, operator. . . .

WOMAN: Lights. . . .

WOMAN: Lights. . . .

MAN: Operator. . . .

MAN: Lights. . . .

MAN: Lights. . . .

WOMAN: Lights. . . .

WOMAN: Lights. . . .

MAN (*German dialect*): Operator, operator, lights. . . .

MAN: Lights, lights. . . .

WOMAN: Lights, lights. . . .

MAN: Operator, operator. . . .

MAN: Operator. . . .

WOMAN: Lights. . . .

WOMAN: Lights. . . .

MAN: Operator. . . .

MAN: Lights. . . .

MAN: Lights. . . .

WOMAN: Lights. . . .

WOMAN: Lights. . . .

MAN: Lights. . . .

MAN: Lights. . . .

WOMAN: Lights. . . .

MAN: Lights. . . .

WOMAN: Lights. . . .

ALL (*ad libbing*): Lights, lights, lights. . . .

Front traveler curtain closes

SCENE TWO
(Inventors)

CHARACTERS

ANNOUNCER
WILLIAM GILBERT (in 1600)
MICHAEL FARADAY (in 1821)
GEORG SIMON OHM (in 1826)
ZENOBE T. GRAMME (in 1873)
THOMAS A. EDISON (in 1879)
FIRST BUSINESS MAN
SECOND BUSINESS MAN
THIRD BUSINESS MAN
FOURTH BUSINESS MAN
FIFTH BUSINESS MAN
SIXTH BUSINESS MAN
LOUDSPEAKER
FINANCIER

LOUDSPEAKER: And that, ladies and gentlemen, is Power! *(Music interlude)* All right, Jack; take it!

(Front spot picks up ANNOUNCER, *left, in front of curtain.)*

ANNOUNCER: Well, now that you've got some idea of what power is, and how much we depend on it, let's go into the question of who started it. Did it just happen all at once, or is it the result of somebody starting something, discovering something, inventing something, to which somebody else added something, and somebody else perfected it a little more, and so on down the line until we came to power as it is known today?

(Spot on ANNOUNCER *goes out. Curtain opens. The stage is set with three cut-out desks, one upstage right, one downstage center, and the other upstage left.)*

LOUDSPEAKER: 1600. William Gilbert publishes the first work on electric and magnetic phenomena, and the philosophy of experimentation.*

(*Lights come up on desk, right.* GILBERT *enters with a book in his hand, crosses to desk where* FARADAY *stands. On desk is a dynamo. Behind them is projected a representation of an early electrical experiment.*)

GILBERT: Nothing is true, nothing lives, until it has been proved. We must make sure before we give it to humanity. (*Hands book to* FARADAY, *who places it on dynamo. The projection dissolves into that of a dynamo.*)

LOUDSPEAKER: 1821. Michael Faraday invents the first instrument to generate electricity—the dynamo.†

(*Light comes up desk, center, and goes out desk, right.* FARADAY *picks up dynamo and book and crosses to desk, center, where* OHM *stands.*)

FARADAY: If it will help humanity, it is good.

(*The projection dissolves into that of another early electrical experiment.*)

LOUDSPEAKER: 1826. Georg Simon Ohm determines the law governing the flow of current.‡

(OHM *takes dynamo from* FARADAY.)

OHM: Now we can control this force to the great gain of the world.

(*Lights go up desk, left, and out desk, center.*)

LOUDSPEAKER: 1873. Zenobe T. Gramme attaches the dynamo to a motor and it works.§

(OHM *crosses to desk left where* GRAMME *stands. The projection dissolves into a picture of an early type of motor.*)

GRAMME: Now we can make it the slave of humanity.

* Hart, Ivor B., *Makers of Science.*
† *Building America*, Vol. 1, No. 6, p. 8.
‡ Hart, Ivor B., *Makers of Science*, p. 240.
§ *Building America*, Vol. 1, No. 6, p. 9.

(EDISON *enters, left, holding an electric bulb* [*old-fashioned type*] *in his hand.*)

LOUDSPEAKER: 1879. Thomas A. Edison invents the first electric light.*

(EDISON *attaches bulb to socket. Crosses down left. Rear curtains close and the projection fades out. Lights come up, down left, as they dim out, up left.*)

EDISON: The happiness of man! I know of no greater service to render during the short time we live! †

(*Enter* SIX BUSINESS MEN *excitedly, left and right. They surround* EDISON. *Their speeches are excited, almost incoherent, but out of the jumble and ad libbing are heard:*)

FIRST MAN: How much does it cost to run?

SECOND MAN: Let me put you into business!

THIRD MAN: Sell me the rights for New York!

FOURTH MAN: Sell me the rights for New Jersey!

FIRST MAN: Sell me the rights for Brooklyn!

FIFTH MAN: Sell me the rights for Harlem!

SIXTH MAN: Sell me the rights for Delaware! (*Out of the welter of ad libbing are heard the words* "money!" "profits," "investment," "corporations," "thousands, millions, billions!" *as they try to wrest the bulb from his hands.* EDISON *stands dazed.*)

LOUDSPEAKER: Just a moment, gentlemen! Aren't you being a bit foolish? This invention is just a drop in the bucket. How much can you make on a little bulb? But the *power* to make it work! That's different.

(*The six who have frozen suddenly come to life. They rush upstage to the desks. Lights come up on all three desks. Each places a small sign on his desk, reading from left to right,* "United States Electric Company," "American Electric Company," "National Lighting Corpora-*

* *Edison at Menlo Park*, published by General Electric Co.
† Miller, F. T., *Thomas Edison*, 1931.

tion," "The International Electric & Fuel Corporation,"
and last, the "Hoboken Electric Company." Each picks
up a telephone from under the desk. During the above:)

LOUDSPEAKER: The New York Stock Exchange is in a panic.
Gas stocks drop and keep on dropping. Shares in the
Edison Electric Company skyrocket from one to five
hundred dollars! *

(Rear curtains open and a panic stock exchange scene is
projected.)

FIRST MAN (into telephone): Get me the mayor's office,
quick. (Punctuating this, the other men speak into telephones: "the mayor's office, get me the mayor," etc., etc.)

LOUDSPEAKER: A record is reached when three shares are
sold for six thousand dollars, resold in a few minutes
for ten thousand dollars, and resold again the same day,
for fifteen thousand dollars.

FIRST MAN (into telephone): Hello, Mr. Mayor? I can supply
electricity to light your streets at the rate of seventy cents
per light per night! †

SECOND MAN (into telephone): I can light every lamp in
New York for fifty-eight cents a night.‡

THIRD MAN: Fifty cents a night.

FOURTH MAN (into telephone): Forty-two and one-half cents
per night! §

FIFTH MAN: Thirty cents a night! ||

SIXTH MAN: Twenty cents! Twenty cents, I said! ¶

TOGETHER: Seventy cents! Fifty-eight cents! Forty-two and
one-half cents! Thirty, thirty, twenty, d'you hear!

(Enter FINANCIER, who comes up center.)

FINANCIER: Come, come, gentlemen, why all this bickering?
Competition in this business is ruinous—to you and to

* Edison at Menlo Park, published by General Electric Co.
† New York Times, May 16, 1887. || Ibid.
‡ Ibid.   ¶ Ibid.
§ Ibid.

the consumer. By sharing the same territory you're duplicating costs and cutting consumption. In your industry, the more electricity sold, the less the cost—to you and to the consumer— Now why don't you let me consolidate your holdings? Let me consolidate them into one big corporation, The Universal Electric Lighting and Fuel Corporation of Hoboken, New Jersey! * (*All business men surround him downstage, center, and hold positions until:*

Blackout

SCENE THREE
(*Consumer—Kilowatt Hour*)

CHARACTERS

LOUDSPEAKER
CONSUMER
ELECTRICIAN
FIRST GROCERY CLERK
SECOND GROCERY CLERK
FIRST BUTCHER
SECOND BUTCHER
MANAGER OF AN ELECTRIC COMPANY

LOUDSPEAKER: Nineteen hundred: Dividends rise, stockholders are happy and electric consumption increases. But where is the man who uses it? Where is this consumer? Let's have a look at him!
(*Arc is played all over stage, searching for* CONSUMER. *It finally picks him out, upstage, right.*)
LOUDSPEAKER: Ah, there he is!

* Note: All names of lighting companies in the foregoing scene, except that of the Edison Electric Company, are fictional and so intended.

(The CONSUMER *is a meek-looking little man dressed in the period. He sits on a chair. The arc should grow larger until it takes in a good part of the stage, and there, tucked away in one little corner, is the* CONSUMER. *When he is finally discovered he gets up and comes downstage, center, and there is projected "C is for Consumer." Front spotlight follows him all through scene.)*

LOUDSPEAKER: What do you pay for electricity, Mister?

CONSUMER: Too much. Seventeen cents a kilowatt hour.*

LOUDSPEAKER: What's a kilowatt hour?

CONSUMER: I don't know. That's what it says on the bill. *(Reads it)* Thirty-nine kilowatt hours at seventeen cents per hour, total six sixty-three.

LOUDSPEAKER: You're paying for it, but you don't know what a kilowatt hour is. How many ounces in a pound?

CONSUMER: Sixteen.

LOUDSPEAKER: How many quarts in a gallon?

CONSUMER: Four.

LOUDSPEAKER: How many inches in a yard?

CONSUMER: Thirty-six.

LOUDSPEAKER: But you don't know what a kilowatt hour is!

CONSUMER: No, I don't, what is it?

LOUDSPEAKER: Well—a kilowatt hour is—a kilowatt is a—eh—uh—

CONSUMER: Go on. I'm listening.

LOUDSPEAKER *(desperately)*: Isn't there *anyone* who knows what a kilowatt hour is?

(Second front spotlight picks up ELECTRICIAN, *up left, and follows him.)*

ELECTRICIAN: I do.

CONSUMER: He's the electrician.

ELECTRICIAN: Yeah, I was up there in the prologue, pullin' them switches. Remember? *(Comes down to* CONSUMER, *center.)*

* Edison Electric Institute *Bulletin* No. 3, June 3, 1936, p. 6.

LOUDSPEAKER: Well—what *is* a kilowatt hour?

ELECTRICIAN (*calling, off*): Hey, Mike! Drop that work light. (*The work light comes down*) Now light it up. Now when this thousand-watt bulb burns for an hour that's a kilowatt hour.

LOUDSPEAKER (*after a pause*): Is that all?

ELECTRICIAN: That's all. The word comes from the Greek, *chilioi,* meaning thousand, and "watt" meaning watt—chilioi-watt or kilowatt. Anything else?

LOUDSPEAKER (*weakly*): No, thank you.

ELECTRICIAN: O.K., Mike, kill it.

(*Work light goes up.* ELECTRICIAN *exits, whistling. The projection becomes "K is for Kilowatt."*)

CONSUMER: Now that I know what it is, I still think I'm paying too much.

LOUDSPEAKER: The company that services you is only making a fair profit.

CONSUMER: What's a fair profit?

LOUDSPEAKER: Six to nine per cent.

CONSUMER: Who said so?

LOUDSPEAKER: The Courts.

CONSUMER: And the bank only gives me three! * What do they do with all that money?

LOUDSPEAKER: It goes back to the stockholders in dividends. (*Pause. The* CONSUMER *picks up his shopping bag and starts off*) Where are you going?

CONSUMER: I've got to do some shopping and I'm going to stop in at the company. I'll tell those people something! Seventeen cents a kilowatt hour!

(*Exits left, and immediately re-enters left. Overhead spot picks out two* GROCERY CLERKS. *They stand beside each other, facing out. They are dressed alike, in aprons. If*

* Wm. B. Dana & Co., *Annual Financial Review,* 1901; also *Public Utility Rate Fixing,* C. E. Grunsky, 1918.

possible they should look alike. Their actions are stylized.
CONSUMER *crosses to* FIRST CLERK.)

CONSUMER: How much are your potatoes?

FIRST CLERK: Fifteen pounds for a quarter.*

CONSUMER: Too high. I'll go some place else. (*Crosses to* SECOND CLERK) How much are your potatoes?

SECOND CLERK: Twenty pounds for a quarter.†

CONSUMER: Fine, I'll take 'em.

(*Light picks up two* BUTCHERS. *He crosses to first one.*)

CONSUMER: How much are pork chops?

FIRST BUTCHER: Twenty cents a pound.

CONSUMER: Too high. I'll go some place else. (*Crosses to* SECOND BUTCHER) How much are pork chops?

SECOND BUTCHER: Fifteen cents a pound.‡

CONSUMER: I'll take 'em.

(*Light comes up on* MANAGER *of electric company seated at cut-out desk.*)

CONSUMER: How much you charging me for electricity?

MANAGER: Seventeen cents a kilowatt hour.§

CONSUMER: Too high. I'll go some place else. (*He crosses and looks around, sees no one*) Where's the other fellow?

MANAGER: There is no other fellow.

(*Projection changes to "M is for Monopoly."*)

CONSUMER: You the only one selling electricity in this city? ‖

MANAGER: That's right.

CONSUMER: And if I don't get it from you I have to do without it?

MANAGER: That's right. Would you like us to discontinue service?

CONSUMER (*apologetically*): Er—no—never mind! (*Runs off.*)

Blackout

---

* U. S. Bureau of Labor Statistics.
† *Ibid.*
‡ *Ibid.*
§ Edison Electric Institute *Bulletin* No. 3. June 3, 1936, p. 3.
‖ *Electrical World & Engineer,* Vol. 35, No. 7, p. 242. Feb. 17, 1900.

SCENE FOUR
(*Expansion*)

CHARACTERS

LOUDSPEAKER
T. COMMERFORD MARTIN

LOUDSPEAKER: New York, June 6, 1905. T. Commerford Martin, Chairman of the Progress Committee of the National Electric Light Association, reports to the convention.*

(*Front spotlight comes up on* MARTIN, *center, standing behind lectern. Behind him is projected a cartoon of a convention banquet.*)

MARTIN: And, gentlemen, enough is not being done to cultivate and create the small consumer. The figures of the New York Edison Company show, roughly, thirty-five thousand customers. Now, that is a good number, but do you believe for one moment that such a figure is the limit of possibilities on Manhattan Island? Electric light and power are falling far short of the ideal in reaching only one-sixth of the population of any given territory. It is to be feared that the public and too many utility companies still regard electric light as a luxury, and the electric motor as costly, and electric heat quite out of reach. This was true once, gentlemen, but is true no longer!

Blackout

* NELA Convention Proceedings, 1905, Vol. 1, p. 17.

SCENE FIVE
(Park Bench—1907)

CHARACTERS

LOUDSPEAKER

MAN ON PARK BENCH

POLICEMAN

LOUDSPEAKER: 1907. Revenues in the electric field reach one hundred seventy million.*

(*A park bench, a* MAN *seated. Beside him stands a* COP *in a uniform of period, 1907. The projection is a New York park scene of the period.*)

MAN (*looks up from paper*): Certainly is a wonderful age we live in.

COP (*eating apple*): Sure.

MAN: Read about this electric convention in Chicago?

COP: Nope! Ain't got time to read. (*He stretches and sits beside* MAN.)

MAN: Fellow named Johnson made a speech.

COP: What about?

MAN: Electricity.

COP: Oh! (*bites apple.*)

MAN: He says some day we're goin' to have electric balloons, submarines and boats.

COP: Yeah?

MAN: Yeah. Another guy said they got an electric railway runnin' up and down the whole pier at Coney Island! Seven hundred feet! (COP *yawns*) Certainly is a wonderful age we live in! Telephones, electric lights, street cars, lamps to keep you hot, and fans to keep you cool. Press a button and an electric knife comes down and cuts your

* Edison Electric Institute, *Statistical Bull.* No. 3, June 1936, p. 10.

paper, somethin' else grabs it and pushes it into the press and, smack, the type comes down, and you're all through for the day!

COP: So you got one of them new-fangled electric presses, eh?

MAN: No. Not me, I can't afford it.

COP: Well, what about these here fans and lamps? They any good?

MAN: How do I know? I ain't never seen one.

COP: You got electric *lights,* haven't you? (COP *rises.*)

MAN: Nope, I live way out in the country—145th Street. Company ain't got up that far yet.

COP (*starting off*): Which way you goin' home, trolley?

MAN: Trolley don't go out that way. Gotta take a horse-car.

COP: Well, so long. Give me a ring some time!

MAN: Can't. Haven't got a phone. (MAN *exits left*) Certainly is a wonderful age we live in!

Curtain

SCENE SIX
(Fair Profits)

CHARACTERS

LOUDSPEAKER

CONSUMER

CHAIRMAN

FIRST DIRECTOR ⎫
SECOND DIRECTOR ⎪
THIRD DIRECTOR ⎬ Board of Directors
FOURTH DIRECTOR ⎭

WITNESS ⎫
FIRST COMMISSIONER ⎬ Utilities Commission
SECOND COMMISSIONER ⎭

MANAGER of Electric Company

(Light on CONSUMER. *He paces back and forth. Suddenly he stops, and points up to the* LOUDSPEAKER. . . .)

CONSUMER *(to* LOUDSPEAKER): Excuse me, can I ask you a few questions? You said the courts allow the company to make a fair profit.

LOUDSPEAKER: Right.

CONSUMER: And a fair profit is anywhere from six to nine per cent.*

LOUDSPEAKER: Right.

CONSUMER: Of what? Six to nine per cent of what?

LOUDSPEAKER: Of their capital account!

CONSUMER: What's that?

LOUDSPEAKER: The amount of their investment, operating expenses, maintenance, and so forth. This determines your electric rates and is known as a rate base.

CONSUMER: I see. Then if their capital account is bigger, my rates go up!

LOUDSPEAKER: Right.

CONSUMER: And if it's smaller? *(Motions downward with his thumb.)*

LOUDSPEAKER: Right again. *(A pause. The* CONSUMER *rubs his chin reflectively; soon a shrewd look appears in his eye.)*

CONSUMER *(hesitantly)*: Of course I don't want to suspect anybody—to me everybody's as honest as the day is long.

LOUDSPEAKER: Of course.

CONSUMER *(very timidly)*: Just the same, would it be all right if I—that is—do you suppose they'd let me have a look at the books—just a quick one?

LOUDSPEAKER: Certainly not! But you can ask the Power Commission for an investigation!

CONSUMER *(joyfully)*: Can I?

LOUDSPEAKER: They just got through with one in New York.

CONSUMER *(excitedly)*: What'd they find?

* *Public Utility Rate Fixing*, C. F. Grunsky, 1918.

LOUDSPEAKER: Oh, a lot of things, but principally the Mack Utility Investigating Committee in New York State found that sometimes . . .*
(*First traveler curtain opens and stage, right, lights up on a Board of Directors.* CHAIRMAN *stands addressing the Board.*)

CHAIRMAN: Gentlemen, our properties have been appraised at four million dollars.

FIRST DIRECTOR (*chuckling*): Well, we haven't depreciated much.

CHAIRMAN: Do you realize this may mean a rate cut? (*The* DIRECTORS *look disturbed.*)

CHAIRMAN: Now I have a proposal. . . . We must hire another firm of appraisers.

SECOND DIRECTOR: And pay another half-million-dollar fee?

CHAIRMAN: Certainly—and more if we have to! Are you forgetting, gentlemen, that our rates are based on what we spend, on our capital account? (*He raps his knuckles on the table. A pause.*)

THIRD DIRECTOR (*who has been thinking, his chin in his hand*): Say, what about those old trucks we've got piled up at Plant 16?

FOURTH DIRECTOR: They won't run any more!

CHAIRMAN (*suavely*): Gentlemen, they have all been included in the rate base—at the price we paid for them.

THIRD DIRECTOR: It seems to me we ought to have some more old junk lying around some place. . . .†
(*Blackout. First traveler curtain closes, leaving* CONSUMER *in front of curtain.*)

CONSUMER (*excitedly*): Did that actually happen?

LOUDSPEAKER: Certainly!

CONSUMER (*excitedly*): You mean they can spend any

* *New York Herald Tribune,* December 19, 1935.
† *New York Times,* February 1, 1935, *et supra.*

amount of money on anything they like and throw in all that old junk besides, and *I* pay for it?

LOUDSPEAKER: It all appears in your rate base.

CONSUMER (*pacing furiously*): I'm going to do something about this!

LOUDSPEAKER: Wait. Listen to this. An expert for the Public Service Corporation of New Jersey is testifying at a Utilities Commission rate hearing.*

(*First traveler curtain opens. Lights on a* WITNESS, *left, talking before two* COMMISSIONERS. *A picture of a hearing room is projected.*)

WITNESS: . . . and I believe this company's rates are justified. It should be remembered that under the company's going values there should be included and capitalized in the rate base the George Washington Bridge, the Holland Tunnel, the highway system of the State and the flourishing birth rate of the thirteen counties which the company serves!

FIRST COMMISSIONER: But the company does not own these things!

SECOND COMMISSIONER: And what has the birth rate to do with electric rates?

WITNESS (*slowly and seriously*): All of these things make a rich territory and the company has every right to levy tribute upon it!

(*Blackout, stage left.* CONSUMER, *stage center, talks to* LOUDSPEAKER.)

CONSUMER: You mean all these things appear in my rate base?

LOUDSPEAKER: Yes.

CONSUMER: And I've got to pay accordingly?

LOUDSPEAKER: Yes.

CONSUMER (*excitedly*): Why—why—why—

* Coleman McAlister, "Victory in New Jersey," *The Nation,* July 31, 1935, p. 133.

(Starts off, right. Lights come up on Electric Company MANAGER *at desk, right.)*

MANAGER: Would you like me to discontinue service?

CONSUMER *(apologetically)*: Oh—er—no—never mind.

Blackout

SCENE SEVEN
(Holding Company)

CHARACTERS

LOUDSPEAKER

MARTIN INSULL

MAN WHO KNOWS

EIGHT STAGEHANDS

GEORGE W. NORRIS, Senator from Nebraska

SHERMAN MINTON, Senator from Indiana

BURTON K. WHEELER, Senator from Montana

THE MESSRS. CARMICHAEL, Director of a Holding Company

ANGUS K. BUTTONKOOPER, a consumer

LOUDSPEAKER: What is a holding company? Martin Insull speaking.

(Lights come up on INSULL, *downstage right.)*

INSULL: To the holding companies is very largely due the credit for the great development of the electric light and power business during the last ten or fifteen years.*

Blackout

LOUDSPEAKER: What is a holding company?

(General lighting comes up on entire stage. MAN *stands, center.)*

* Federal Trade Commission, Vol. 71-A, p. 310.

MAN WHO KNOWS: I'll show you. (*To someone off stage left*) Hey, Charlie, bring on that pile of boxes.
(*Three* STAGEHANDS *enter, each carries a large wooden box, and sets it down. Two of the boxes—blue—are square, and the other—yellow—is rectangular and a little larger. The* STAGEHANDS *set down the blue boxes, side by side.*)

LOUDSPEAKER: What are those?

MAN WHO KNOWS (*to assistants*): Stick around, I'll need you. (*to* LOUDSPEAKER) Now, imagine this box and this box (*pointing to the blue boxes*) are operating companies.

LOUDSPEAKER: Go ahead!

MAN WHO KNOWS: These two companies generate electricity and transport it by means of poles and wires, and so forth, to consumers in different sections of the country. They have no connection with each other. Both of them need expansion.

LOUDSPEAKER: But I asked about holding companies.

MAN WHO KNOWS: Hold your horses. I am coming to that. This is where the holding company comes in. (*To an assistant*) Hand me that box. . . . Thank you. (*He places the third box—yellow, rectangular—on the first two boxes, linking them to make a pyramid*) Now, this holding company (*pointing to the yellow box*) buys up the common stock of the two operating companies (*pointing to the blue boxes*) and extends to them the finances they need.*

LOUDSPEAKER: I see. It puts up the money.

MAN WHO KNOWS: Well, not always.

LOUDSPEAKER: What else does a holding company do?

MAN WHO KNOWS: It is supposed to cut down the cost of overhead. Sometimes it provides a joint generating plant. Usually it pools the engineering and construction services.†

* Federal Trade Commission, Vol. 72-A, pp. 118-19. † *Ibid.*, p. 195.

LOUDSPEAKER: So that's a holding company. Thank you very much, and now we'll . . .

MAN WHO KNOWS: Wait a minute. You haven't seen anything yet.

LOUDSPEAKER: What's that?

MAN WHO KNOWS: I say, there's more to this holding company business. (*To someone off stage, right*) Hey, Joe, bring over that other set of boxes, will you?

(*Three* STAGEHANDS *enter, each carries a large wooden box, and sets it down. Two of the boxes—blue—are square, and the other—yellow—is rectangular, and a little larger. The* STAGEHANDS *set down the blue boxes, left, next to the first set of blue boxes. Two* STAGEHANDS *follow with a long box—orange. This box is approximately three times as long as the first boxes are. The* MAN *pyramids the second yellow box on the second set of blue.*)

MAN WHO KNOWS: Now here's another group of operating companies with holding company. . . . See. (*He points to second set of boxes*) Operating company, operating company, holding company. (*Points to first set of boxes*) Operating company, operating company, holding company. (*To last two* STAGEHANDS) Now hand me that long box! (STAGEHANDS *help him place the long orange box on top of the two pyramids, linking them together.*)

MAN WHO KNOWS (*continuing*): Now here is the top holding company.

LOUDSPEAKER: What does *it* do?

MAN WHO KNOWS: Well, it bears the same relation to these sub-holding companies that they bear to . . .

LOUDSPEAKER (*interrupting*): Oh, so now they've become sub-holding companies.

MAN WHO KNOWS: Oh, that isn't anything. When I get through piling up these boxes, those things (*indicating*) will be just sub-sub-sub-holding companies.

LOUDSPEAKER: I think we get the idea, if it's all the same to you.

MAN WHO KNOWS: If I can't show you, you had better listen to Senator Norris over here.

Blackout

(*Lights come up on* SENATOR NORRIS, *left.*)

SENATOR NORRIS: Scientific ingenuity has demonstrated that, in the electric world, to get the most economical results, we must have monopoly. But when electricity becomes common in every house, and as necessary as water to drink, if we are subjected to the will of a great monopoly that reaches from the Canadian boundary to the Gulf of Mexico, and from ocean to ocean, we will become in reality, slaves. . . .* I desire to show the Senate today . . . (*Scrim comes down in front of* NORRIS. *On it, near top center, is projected a spread-eagle*) . . . by a few charts and illustrations, the absurdities into which the holding company leads, not only as it concerns the consumers of electricity, but also the honest investors in securities.†

LOUDSPEAKER: Senator Sherman Minton of Indiana.

(*Lights come up on* MINTON, *right.*)

SENATOR MINTON: Isn't it true, Senator, that, from the standpoint of those who have organized and control the holding companies, the higher they pyramid them, the less money it takes at the top, to control the entire structure? ‡

SENATOR NORRIS: It is. This is the universal rule, running all through these corporations, from one end of the United States to another. They are interlocked, intermingled, intertwined, interwoven, mixed up, scrambled

* *Congressional Record,* February 29, March 5 and 9, 1928.
† *Congressional Record,* June 3, 1935, p. 34.
‡ *Ibid.,* p. 34.

and all put together so that they are practically like one man, levying upon everybody who uses electric light or electric power in this country. (*Lights go out, right.* MINTON *exits*) Now I want to devote just a little time to the officers and directors of these corporations. Take the case of Mr. C. E. Groesbeck, for instance.* He is Chairman of the Board and director of the Electric Bond and Share Company. (*The eagle fades and an animated chart showing an octopus progresses on the scrim*) He is Chairman of the Board and director of American Investors, Incorporated, and the American Gas and Electric Company. He is Chairman of the Board and director of the American and Foreign Power Company, and the American Power and Light Company. He is a director of the Carolina Power and Light Company, the Cuban Electric Company, and the Mississippi River Fuel Corporation. He is Chairman of the Board and director of the Lehigh Power Securities Corporation. He is Chairman of the Board and director of the Electric Power and Light Corporation. He is Chairman of the Board and director of the United Gas Corporation. He is a director of the Pennsylvania Power and Light Corporation. He is a director of the Tri-Continental Corporation, the Havana Electric and Utilities Company, the Utah Power and Light Company, and the Phoenix Utilities Corporation. In addition, he is a director or other officer in thirty-two corporations scattered all over the world! (*The octopus movie holds and is static.*)

LOUDSPEAKER: Senator Burton K. Wheeler of Montana.

(WHEELER *enters, left.*)

WHEELER: In other words, when the Electric Bond and Share Company makes a contract with, say, the Florida Power and Light Company, the same officer who repre-

* *Ibid.*

sents the Electric Bond and Share Company also represents the operating company, and when contracts are
made, the same man signs the contracts for both
parties? *

SENATOR NORRIS: What you say, Senator, is absolutely true.

WHEELER: Then this puts a director in the *almost impossible position* of sitting across the table from himself and
signing the contracts for the holding company and for
all the different operating companies?

SENATOR NORRIS: That is correct.

LOUDSPEAKER: An *almost* impossible position. . . .

*(Lights go out on WHEELER and NORRIS. Scrim goes up.
Lights come up on CARMICHAEL seated at cut-out desk,
right. Left of desk is an empty chair. During the following, flesh-pink light is on CARMICHAEL when he sits at
desk, which changes to steel-blue when he moves to chair,
desk left. There is projected behind him a cartoon of a
triple mirror.)*

CARMICHAEL: † Mr. Carmichael, I've got a couple of propositions for you, good propositions, that can only result
in great benefit to your company, your stockholders and
your consumers. . . . Now one of our subsidiaries is the
Great Southwestern Engineering Company. I want them
to look over your plant and give you some advice on
how to economize on your transmission system. This
service will cost you fifty thousand a year. *(He rises from
desk, and changes to chair left, lights on him changing)*
Fifty thousand! That's a lot of money for a small plant
like ours, Mr. Carmichael. But if you say so, I guess it's
worth it. . . . Where do I sign? *(Takes pen from desk
and signs contract lying on desk.)*

LOUDSPEAKER: Now this service may be worth fifty thousand

* *Congressional Record*, May 31 to June 14, 1935 (one volume).
† This character is fictional.

a year or fifty cents. Nobody knows but Mr. Carmichael,
and he won't tell.

CARMICHAEL (*changing to chair at desk*): Now, Mr. Carmichael, I've got something that's really going to interest
you, something extra special. You know that piece of
real estate in your town that I own? (*Changes to chair,
left*) You mean that one down by the river you paid a
hundred thousand for and got stuck? (*He laughs.
Changes to chair at desk*) Yes, that's the one. You'll need
it for that new plant you're going to build. I'll tell you
about that later. My price is a hundred and fifty
thousand, Mr. Carmichael. (*Emphatically*) And you can't
afford to turn it down. (*Changes to chair, left*) A hundred
and fifty thousand! Well, maybe you're right, Mr. Carmichael. Where do I sign? (*He signs and changes to chair
at desk.*)

LOUDSPEAKER: Maybe he is right, but nobody will ever
know but Mr. Carmichael.

CARMICHAEL: And now I'm going to let you into a little
secret. Mr. Carmichael, I've decided to merge your company with National Electric! (*Changes to chair, left.
From here on action speeds up*) National Electric! Why,
they've been losing money for years! (*Changes*) I know
it. That's why I'm doing it. (*Changes*) But that'll pull
my profit sheet all the way down! (*Changes*) Those are
my orders, Mr. Carmichael. (*Changes*) But, Mr. Carmichael . . . ? (*Changes—and coldly*) Yes, Mr. Carmichael? (*Changes*) Oh, never mind. . . . Where do I
sign? (*Signs and then starts mopping his brow, exhausted
from his exertion. As he does this, spotlight picks up* CON-
SUMER *entering, left.* CARMICHAEL *changes back to desk,
and flesh-pink light stays on him throughout remainder
of scene.* CONSUMER *walks across stage timidly, looking
around to see if he's in the right place. He crosses to
desk.*)

CONSUMER (*removing hat*): Mr. Carmichael?

CARMICHAEL: Yes?

CONSUMER (*very timidly*): Can—I—just—talk to you for a minute?

CARMICHAEL: Who're you?

CONSUMER: My name is Angus K. Buttonkooper.* I'm a consumer.

CARMICHAEL (*His manner changes; he becomes jovial*): Certainly, Mr. Buttonkooper. Sit right down. Have a cigar! (*Hands cigar to* CONSUMER) Now what can I do for you?

CONSUMER: I think my rates are too high!

CARMICHAEL: That's the proper spirit, Mr. Buttonkooper. I admire a man who'll stand up and fight when he thinks he's been stepped on. (CONSUMER *grins*) Did you know we just entered into a contract with the Great Southwestern Engineering Corporation? They're going to teach us how to economize.

CONSUMER (*grinning*): That's nice.

CARMICHAEL: It'll cost us fifty thousand a year. (CONSUMER'S *grin dies*) And we've finally succeeded in closing the deal for a piece of property we've been needing a long time. It took a great deal of persuasion, Mr. Buttonkooper, a great deal of persuasion, but we finally landed it. That's a hundred and fifty thousand more. (CONSUMER'S *face grows longer*) Incidentally, did you read that the company is in such a bad shape that we had to float a million-dollar bond issue? (*Nodding vigorously, as* CONSUMER *just stares at him*) It's all in the papers, Mr. Buttonkooper, it's all in the papers. . . . Now there's been a movement among some of our officers to—to . . . (*He stops and regards* CONSUMER, *who awaits the news fearfully*) . . . but I don't think you have to worry, Mr. Buttonkooper. . . .

* Fictional character.

CONSUMER (*with a sigh of relief*): You mean you won't raise my rates to pay for all this?

CARMICHAEL: Not one red cent. Our company realizes its obligation to its consumers.

CONSUMER: Thank you. Thank you. . . .

CARMICHAEL: Good day, Mr. Buttondropper, Mr. Buttondripper, Mr. . . .

(CONSUMER *starts to exit, but comes back and returns cigar to* CARMICHAEL.)

Blackout

LOUDSPEAKER: Senator George W. Norris of Nebraska.

(*Lights come up on* NORRIS, *left.*)

NORRIS: Everything that is produced by electric power has contributed to it. Every common little home must make its contribution and every big factory! In the end it all comes out of the consumers, the common people of the United States! In my opinion the holding company constitutes the greatest evil of the civilized age! *

Blackout

SCENE EIGHT †
(*Childish Questions*)

CHARACTERS

A MAN
HIS DAUGHTER

LOUDSPEAKER: 1912. Revenues in the electric field reach two hundred eighty-five million.‡

* *Congressional Record*, May 31 to June 14, 1935 (one volume).
† Note: This entire scene is fictional.
‡ Edison Electric Institute *Bulletin* No. 3, June 1936, p. 10.

(Lights up on FATHER *and* DAUGHTER, *center. He is seated in chair; she is sitting on the floor playing with large alphabet blocks. Projection represents a Christmas tree and teddy bear.)*

GIRL: Daddy, where do we get electricity from?

FATHER *(annoyed at the interruption)*: We get it from the electric company.

GIRL: Where does the company get it?

FATHER: They generate it.

GIRL: What's "generate" mean?

FATHER: Generate means . . . means . . . can't you see Daddy is busy? Why don't you play with your blocks, dear?

GIRL: How do they generate it, Daddy?

FATHER: Oh. . . . *(under his breath)* Damn! Sometimes they run dynamos with steam engines and sometimes they run dynamos with water.

GIRL: What is a dynamo?

FATHER: Well, a dynamo is . . . What the devil do you want to know that for?

GIRL *(after a pause)*: I know. A dynamo is what they make electricity with. We had that in school.

FATHER: Well, why didn't you get the rest in school?

GIRL: What would happen if the company wouldn't give us electricity any more?

FATHER: We'd be in a hell of a fix.

GIRL: Then why doesn't the Government give us electricity?

FATHER: Because it would be competing with private business, and, besides, everybody knows that the Government wouldn't be efficient.

GIRL *(pauses, apparently thinking)*: Daddy, who runs the Post Office?

FATHER: The Government runs the Post Office.

GIRL: Why does the Government run the Post Office?

FATHER: Because it's too important to us to permit any-body else to run it.

GIRL: Well, Daddy, don't you think electricity is important? You said we'd be in a hell of a fix if the company quit giving it to us.

FATHER: Watch your language, young lady!

GIRL: It was what you said, Daddy.

FATHER: The Post Office and electric lights are different.

GIRL (stands up, holding the blocks in her arm): Daddy, who is the Government?

FATHER: The Government is you and me, I guess—the people.

GIRL: Do all the people need electricity?

FATHER: Yes.

GIRL: And does the company own what all the people need?

FATHER: That's right!

GIRL: Gee, Daddy; the people are awfully dumb. (She drops the blocks.)

Blackout

SCENE NINE
(Insull's Empire)

CHARACTERS

LOUDSPEAKER
SAMUEL J. INSULL
CONSUMER-INVESTOR

LOUDSPEAKER: A lesson in high finance. Presenting Samuel J. Insull of Chicago.

(*Light comes up on* INSULL *and* CONSUMER-INVESTOR, *seated center.*)

INSULL: Now, son, just sit still and watch me and I'm going to show you how to make a lot of money.

CONSUMER-INVESTOR: What do I have to do?

INSULL: Just keep quiet and when I need you I'll let you know.

LOUDSPEAKER: Samuel J. Insull organizes the Middle West Utilities Company, president, Samuel J. Insull, capitalization nothing, assets nothing, holdings nothing. Samuel J. Insull sells the Middle West Utilities Company, president, Samuel J. Insull, $330,000 worth of securities.*
(*A projection of a stock certificate appears—as* INSULL *takes securities out of his pocket.*)

CONSUMER-INVESTOR: Don't be a sucker. They haven't got any dough!

INSULL: Quiet! (*He transfers securities from coat pocket on his right side to pocket on left side.*)

LOUDSPEAKER: To raise the money to pay Samuel J. Insull, the Middle West Utilities Company issues ten million dollars' worth of stock, all of which the Middle West Utilities Company, Samuel J. Insull, president, sells to Samuel J. Insull for $3,600,000.†

CONSUMER-INVESTOR (*as* INSULL *takes stocks from his pants pocket and transfers them to his coat*): There's something funny going on here.

LOUDSPEAKER: But Samuel Insull hasn't got a nickel in the world to pay for these stocks.

INSULL (*turns to* CONSUMER-INVESTOR, *smiling*): Now, son, I'd like to talk to you.

CONSUMER-INVESTOR: Who, *me?*

INSULL: You know, I've sort of liked you from the first day I laid eyes on you.

CONSUMER-INVESTOR: What is this, a touch?

INSULL: What kind of car do you drive, son?

CONSUMER-INVESTOR: A Chevrolet. Why?

---

* "Up and Down with Insull," *Collier's,* December 17, 1932.
† *Ibid.*

INSULL: How would you like to own a sixteen-cylinder Cadillac, all new and shiny, with a footman and a chauffeur? (CONSUMER-INVESTOR *regards him ecstatically.*)

INSULL: How would you like to exchange that little house of yours for a real home on Long Island, with one hundred and sixty-eight rooms, a string of polo ponies and nine swimming pools? (*During the above, the* CONSUMER-INVESTOR *becomes more and more interested; he nods, a big grin on his face.*)

INSULL: How would you like to go around the world, Cathay, Mocha and Java, on your own yacht—the biggest in the world—with your wife and kids following you, each one with a yacht of his own, just a wee bit smaller than yours? (*The* CONSUMER-INVESTOR *nods more eagerly.*)

INSULL: How would you like to go up to your boss and say, "Mr. Simmons, I quit. I'm tired of being a wage slave for guys like you to kick around. I invested my money judiciously, I did, and from now on I'm going to live on the dividends from my stocks in the Middle West Utilities Company!" (*The* CONSUMER-INVESTOR *nods as though his head were coming off*) You're a smart boy, son, and I like you. And I want you to know I wouldn't cheat you for the world.

LOUDSPEAKER: Samuel J. Insull sells half his shares to the public for four million dollars, which he hands over to Middle West Utilities Company.* (CONSUMER-INVESTOR *hands* INSULL *money in exchange for stocks.*)

INSULL (*stuffing money in all his pockets as* CONSUMER-INVESTOR *regards stocks*): That's right, look at the pretty pictures.

CONSUMER-INVESTOR (*eagerly*): How much is the dividend going to be, Sam?

INSULL: Well, that depends on how much we make.

* "Up and Down with Insull," *Collier's*, December 17, 1932.

CONSUMER-INVESTOR: How do we know how much we make?

INSULL: Why, I write it down in the books.

CONSUMER-INVESTOR: Can anybody look at the books?

INSULL: Oh, no. This is a holding company. We don't have to show our books to anybody.

CONSUMER-INVESTOR: Who decides how we're going to invest our money?

INSULL: I do.

CONSUMER-INVESTOR: Who decides how much your salary's going to be?

INSULL: I do.

CONSUMER-INVESTOR: And who decides if you're going to give yourself a bonus?

INSULL: I do.

CONSUMER-INVESTOR: Why?

INSULL: Why? Because I still own fifty per cent of the shares in this company and that gives me a controlling interest.

CONSUMER-INVESTOR: You mean the company that I put into business with my four million?

INSULL: That's right.

CONSUMER-INVESTOR: Well, how much have you got invested in it?

INSULL: *Not one red cent!*

Blackout

SCENE TEN
(*Cost Comparison: 1913-1926*)

CHARACTERS

LOUDSPEAKER
MR. LANE, Utilities Official
WOMAN—MRS. LANE—1913   (Right)
WOMAN—MRS. LANE—1926   (Left)

POWER

CLERK	First Pair	(Right)
CLERK	Fruit Counters	(Left)
CLERK	Second Pair	(Right)
CLERK	Hardware	(Left)
CLERK	Third Pair	(Right)
CLERK	Dry Goods	(Left)
FIRST MAN	Fourth Pair	(Right)
SECOND MAN	Rent Collectors	(Left)
CLERK	Fifth Pair	(Right)
CLERK	Electric Company Office	(Left)

LOUDSPEAKER: In the United States the average domestic rate per kilowatt hour in 1926 was 7.4 cents.* In the province of Ontario, Canada, where the system is publicly owned and operated, the average cost per kilowatt hour is 1.66 cents.† This represents a saving to the consumer of . . .

(LANE *enters, right, picked up by spotlight from front. Crosses to center as he talks to* LOUDSPEAKER.)

LANE: ‡ Just a minute, you! Seems to me you've been having a pretty good time showing up us utilities, lettin' everybody see just what you want 'em to see and no more! Now I'm goin' to have my say and some people are goin' to be just a *little bit* surprised! (*Waves his arms*) Come here, girls.

(*Spotlights pick up two women who enter from left and right. One is about twenty-two, dressed in the period of 1913. The other, about thirty-five, is dressed in the period of 1926. A projected dotted line divides the rear curtain, with "1913" blazoned on the right, and "1926" on the left.*)

LANE: Now this is my wife as she looked in 1913, when we

* *Electrical World,* January 7, 1928.
† *What Price Electricity to Our Homes,* Morris L. Cooke.
‡ This character is fictional.

got married, and this is my wife today in 1926. (*He takes money from pocket and hands some to each*) All right, girls. Go out and do your shopping.

(*General lighting comes up on entire stage. At right, running to center, are three separate counters, selling respectively, fruit, household furnishings and clothing. At center is a cage marked* ELECTRIC COMPANY—CASHIER. *This cage has two compartments. At left are three more counters selling the same articles. Behind the three stalls at right, and right half of cage, are clerks dressed in the period of 1913. At left, and left half of cage, clerks are dressed in manner of 1926. During the above* LANE *sits in chair, right, and smilingly looks on. The women stand undecided before fruit counters, left and right.*)

LANE (*from seat*): How about some oranges, dear? We didn't have any for breakfast. (*Both* WOMEN *pick up oranges.*)

CLERK [*right*]: Oranges, madam? Twenty-five cents a dozen.*

CLERK [*left*]: Oranges, madam? Forty-two cents a dozen.

WOMAN [*right*]: I'll take a dozen.

WOMAN [*left*]: I'll take a dozen.

LANE (*as* CLERKS *wrap oranges, turns to audience*): Observe, ladies and gentlemen. From 1913 to 1926, an increase of seventeen cents or sixty-six per cent. (*The* WOMEN *move to next counter*) Why not get that new frying pan you've been talking about for months now? (*Both* WOMEN *pick up frying pans.*)

CLERK [*right*]: That's an excellent frying pan, madam. Fifty cents.

CLERK [*left*]: That's an excellent frying pan, madam, ninety-eight cents.

WOMAN [*right*]: I'll take it.

WOMAN [*left*]: I'll take it.

* *Journal of Commerce,* March 1, 1913 and 1926.

LANE (*to audience*): From fifty to ninety-eight cents—an increase of ninety-six per cent. (*The* WOMEN *move to next counter.*)

LANE (*to* WOMEN): You may as well get me some socks while you're at it. (*Rises.* WOMEN *examine socks.*)

CLERK [*right*]: Those are lisle, madam. Thirty-five cents a pair.

CLERK [*left*]: Those are lisle, madam. Fifty-nine cents a pair.

WOMAN [*right*]: I'll take three pairs.

WOMAN [*left*]: I'll take three pairs.

LANE (*to audience as* WOMEN *take the package*): Fifty-nine over thirty-five. An increase of almost seventy per cent.
(WOMEN *remain at dry goods counters, left and right center respectively; two* MEN *enter left and right. They cross to* WOMEN.)

FIRST MAN (*to* WOMAN [*right*]): Good morning, Mrs. Lane.

SECOND MAN (*to* WOMAN [*left*]): Good morning, Mrs. Lane.

FIRST MAN: Everything all right with the apartment? We had an awful time getting that color you wanted on the walls.

SECOND MAN: Everything all right with the apartment? We had an awful time getting that color you wanted on the walls.

LANE (*as* WOMEN *stand immobile*): Go on, dear. He's waiting for the rent. (WOMAN [*right*] *takes bills from purse and hands them to man.* WOMAN [*left*] *does the same.*)

MAN [*right*] (*counting bills*): Fifty-five dollars. Thank you, Mrs. Lane.

MAN [*left*]: Ninety dollars. Thank you, Mrs. Lane.

MAN [*right*]: Good day, Mrs. Lane.

MAN [*left*]: Good day, Mrs. Lane. (MEN *exit right and left.* LANE *crosses to center and addresses audience.*)

LANE: Sixty-two per cent increase in rent for the same apartment. Now watch this carefully, everybody. (*To* LOUD-SPEAKER) And you, too, up there. Don't anyone miss a word. (*Turns to* WOMEN) Pay your electric bills, dear. (WOMEN *go to cashier windows, center.*)

CLERK [*right*] (*as* WOMAN *pays*): That's right, four dollars and thirty-five cents.

CLERK [*left*] (*as* WOMAN *pays*): That's right, three dollars and seventy cents.

LANE (*to audience, excitedly*): Did you hear that? Three seventy over four-thirty-five, showing, in the face of increases of from sixty-two to ninety-eight per cent in essentials like food, household goods, clothing and rent,* a decrease in the cost of electricity of almost fifteen per cent.† Fifteen per cent! (*To* LOUDSPEAKER) *Put that in your pipe and smoke it!* (*He starts off*) Come on, girls, we're going home.

LOUDSPEAKER: Just a moment, Mr. Lane. Aren't you forgetting something?

LANE (*not quite hearing*): What's that?

LOUDSPEAKER: I said, didn't you forget something?

LANE: Not that I can think of.

LOUDSPEAKER: Isn't it true that the more electricity you sell, the cheaper its cost? And isn't it true that the domestic consumption of electricity has gone up something like four hundred and thirty-five per cent since 1913? ‡

LANE: Well, yes, only . . .

LOUDSPEAKER: And isn't it true that engineering advances from 1913 to 1926 have reduced the operating expenses for one domestic kilowatt hour forty-one per cent? §

LANE: Yes, but . . .

LOUDSPEAKER: And isn't it true that the gross domestic revenues went up two hundred and seventy-five per cent? ‖

* *World Almanac,* 1936, p. 364.
† Based on figures from *Electrical World,* January 7, 1928.
‡ *Ibid.*
§ *Ibid.*
‖ *Ibid.*

LANE: Yes, yes, yes.

LOUDSPEAKER: And that is why, Mr. Lane, we say that, judging from your cost sheets, though your rates have gone down, *they have not gone down nearly enough!* Good day, Mr. Lane.

(LANE *takes the* WOMEN *by the arm and starts off, left.*)

Blackout

SCENE ELEVEN
(Consumer Sues)

CHARACTERS

CONSUMER
LOUDSPEAKER

(*Music interlude. Enter* CONSUMER, *left. Instead of his normal, timid self, he has become a roaring lion. He crosses, full of determination, his shoulders high. The projection becomes a cartoon of Justice over a prizefight ring.*)

CONSUMER: I'm sick and tired of all this kickin' around. Every time they want to take a sock at somebody, I'm the guy that gets it. First it was that monopoly business. Then it was the rate base. Then it was the holding company. On top of that, stocks go up but I can't squawk because what would happen to the poor little widows and orphans that eke out a *bare existence* on their dividends! I say, to hell with 'em; I'm goin' to fight! (*Takes off coat and hat and drops them on floor.*)

LOUDSPEAKER: December 28, 1929—Long Island consumers file a petition for lower rates against the Long Island Lighting Company.* (CONSUMER *begins to shadow box.*)

* Public Service Commission, New York, N. Y.

48 POWER

January 27, 1930—the Company answers. The case is argued. (CONSUMER *throws out blows left and right*.)
LOUDSPEAKER *(continuing)*: The Company wins an injunction. (CONSUMER *takes a haymaker and sits down hard. He shakes his head to clear it, then:*)
CONSUMER *(philosophically)*: Oh, well, what did I lose?
LOUDSPEAKER: Plenty.
CONSUMER: Huh?
LOUDSPEAKER: That case cost the company two million, two hundred thousand dollars to fight. It's appearing in your rate base next year.*
CONSUMER *(groaning)*: Oooooh! (*He keels over.*)

Blackout

SCENE TWELVE
(Propaganda)

CHARACTERS

LOUDSPEAKER
A—EDITORS
  MAN, Utilities representative
  EDITOR, Small-town paper
  J. L. MURPHY, Representative of Georgia Railway and Power Company
B—UTILITIES INFORMATION
  WILLARD COPE, Executive Secretary of Georgia Utilities Information Committee
  ROBERT E. HEALY, Counsel Federal Trade Commission
  M. H. AYLESWORTH
C—COLLEGE PROFESSORS
  SIX COLLEGE PROFESSORS

* *New York Times,* February 9, 1935, p. 1, col. 1.

D—SENATOR GEORGE W. NORRIS
SENATOR GEORGE W. NORRIS OF NEBRASKA

SCENE TWELVE—A
(*Editors*)

LOUDSPEAKER: According to the Federal Trade Commission Report, the public utilities spend twenty-five million dollars every year on propaganda and publicity. Twenty-five million dollars! *
(*Lights up on small-town* EDITOR *and utilities representative, left. Desk, two chairs, etc. Projection of presses.*)

MAN: † Your paper's a darn good one, Mr. Bigbee, and honest, too. And the farmers in four counties around here swear by it like they do the Bible. And by the way . . . (*He stops and points to paper spread out on desk*) . . . there's a letter in here some place about electric rates being too high and that the Government ought to do something about it. . . .

EDITOR: ‡ Yeah, that's from Joe Bailey. He's one of our subscribers. He's hepped on the subject of Government ownership.

MAN: Of course what he says is just plain silly. He doesn't know the facts in the case at all. But we're going to answer it just the same.

EDITOR: I'll be glad to print a letter from you, Mr. Crane.

MAN: My company doesn't write letters, Mr. Bigbee. We're going to answer that with a full page ad!

EDITOR (*happily*): A full page ad!

* Federal Trade Commission Report, Vol. 71-A, p. 60.
† Fictional character, scene based on report of Federal Trade Commission.
‡ *Ibid.*

MAN (*rises*): That's right, a full page. I'll have the copy over here tomorrow.

EDITOR: I certainly do appreciate this, Mr. Crane.*

MAN: Forget it. (*Starts off, stops*) Oh, by the way. Since we're paying out so much money to answer that letter, anything you publish in the future should be in the form of paid advertisements, too; they pay to squawk and we pay to answer 'em. That's only fair, isn't it?

EDITOR: It seems fair, only . . .

MAN: There'll be a clause to that effect in our contract.

EDITOR: But people like Joe Bailey haven't got any money. They can't afford to pay for an ad!

MAN: Can't they?

EDITOR: And then their letters won't appear at all!

MAN: Won't they? (*Pause, as he regards him significantly*) So long, Mr. Bigbee.

Blackout

LOUDSPEAKER: According to the Federal Trade Commission Report, Mr. J. L. Murphy, of the Georgia Railway and Power Company, says . . .

(*Lights come up on* MURPHY *down right.*)

MURPHY: The result of our efforts is that out of two hundred and fifty newspapers in Georgia, only four will publish anything at all from the public ownership people! †

Blackout

* Fictitious name.
† Raushenbush, H. S., *High Power Propaganda*, p. 11.

SCENE TWELVE—B
(*Utilities Information*)

LOUDSPEAKER: Mr. Willard Cope, Executive Secretary of the Georgia Utilities Information Committee, is interrogated by the Federal Trade Commission. Counsel, Robert E. Healy . . .*

(*Lights come up on* COPE *seated in chair. Beside him stands* HEALY. *Behind them is projected a heavily draped window, with the capitol dome showing in the distance.*)

HEALY: Mr. Cope, why were the records we asked for destroyed?

COPE (*unruffled, a bit debonair*): Oh, we just didn't want them kicking around the office, that's all.

HEALY: Now in reference to this propaganda and information . . .

COPE (*breaking in*): Mr. Commissioner, my organization has done nothing in the six years I have been with it that can be called propaganda for the utilities or anybody else!

HEALY: Then how do you explain this voucher showing that you paid for subscriptions to the *Columbus Enquirer-Sun* of Columbus, Georgia, a newspaper which has consistently upheld the utilities and attacked any form of Government supervision or control? Now, isn't it true, Mr. Cope, that these subscriptions were sent by you to a great number of consumers of electricity? (*A pause, as* COPE *doesn't answer*) Well, Mr. Cope, have you no answer to this charge?

COPE (*painfully*): I—I—did it in order to raise the general level of the intelligence of the State! That's all!

Blackout

* *New York Times,* May 11, 1928.

LOUDSPEAKER: At a meeting of the Public Relations Section of the Southeast Division of the National Electric Light Association, M. H. Aylesworth, Managing Director, remarked . . .

(*Lights come up on* AYLESWORTH, *right.*)

AYLESWORTH: All the money being spent is worth while. Don't be afraid of the expense. *The public pays!* *

Blackout

SCENE TWELVE—C
(*College Professors*)

LOUDSPEAKER: In the colleges. . . . The following members of a notoriously underpaid profession find extra-curricular employment as lecturers, editors, and advisers for public utility corporations. . . .

(*General lighting on whole stage in blue. Projection is a light bulb with mortar-board cap. The* PROFESSORS, *as their colleges are called, enter, one by one. Each wears a cap and gown, and is reading a book, greatly absorbed. They do not stop, but continue walking. As they enter, left and right, they cross each other. As the entrances are made from various depths of the stage, a formation is achieved of lines crisscrossing. Special music with a college flavor adds to effectiveness of this scene.*)

LOUDSPEAKER: A professor from Rensselaer Polytechnic Institute—eight thousand dollars; a professor from Yale—eight thousand one hundred and seven dollars and twenty-five cents; Professor E. T., unattached—five thousand dollars; a professor from Texas A. and M., three thousand three hundred dollars; a professor from Louisiana State University—ten thousand dollars; a dean from

* Federal Trade Commission Report, Vol. 71-A, p. 60.

Ohio State University—fifteen thousand dollars. . . . These among hundreds of others were reported by the Federal Trade Commission Investigation.* It is also reported that thirty-five million dollars of Harvard funds are invested in utilities securities. . . .† Now these men are entrusted with the education of a nation. Will they tell the *whole story* to their students, and jeopardize their incomes and their university endowments? Let's ask them. . . . Gentlemen . . . (*They all stop still and close their books*) . . . gentlemen—what do you think of the doctrine of municipal ownership? (*In unison, mournfully, they all shake their heads, indicating that they consider it entirely hopeless.* LOUDSPEAKER, *continuing:*) What do you think of Government supervision and control of the abuses we have shown to exist in the public utilities? (*Again they shake their heads*) What do you think of a nice juicy steak smothered in onions? (*The* PROFESSORS *nod their heads energetically, with broad grins on their faces and very much interested.*)

Blackout

SCENE TWELVE—D
(*Senator George W. Norris*)

LOUDSPEAKER: Senator Norris.
(*Lights come up on* NORRIS, *center. Behind him is projected a view of the Senate.*)
SENATOR NORRIS: They have undertaken to control legislatures, public service commissions, members of Congress, school boards, municipal authorities, commercial clubs, secret societies, women's clubs—even Boy Scout organizations. . . . No one would find fault if these influences

* Federal Trade Commission Report, Vol. 71-A, pp. 426-37.
† Federal Trade Commission Report, Vol. 71-A, pp. 174-75.

were operating in public—out in the open! But these emissaries were not known by the people who heard them—or read them. . . .*

Blackout

SCENE THIRTEEN
(*"Get Norris"*)

CHARACTERS

LOUDSPEAKER
GROCERY CLERK
POLITICIAN

LOUDSPEAKER: The word goes out, "Get Norris!"—Broken Bow, Nebraska, 1930. A gentleman does a little shopping.†
(*Light up on the counter of a grocery store, right, at which stands a clerk. Projection is a grocery window.* POLITICIAN *enters.*)

GROCER: What can I do for you, sir?

POLITICIAN: Oh, nothing much. I'll just look around a little. (*Picks up an apple*) Nice-looking apples.

GROCER: Yes, sir. Them's McIntoshes. Good for cookin' and eatin'.

POLITICIAN: You don't say. (*Pause*) How's business?

GROCER: Not so good. Looks like a hard winter comin' on.

POLITICIAN: Seems to me there's always a way for a smart man to help things along a little.

GROCER: How do you mean, bootleg?

POLITICIAN (*laughing*): No, of course not I mean some-

* *The Nation,* September 18, 1929.
† *New York Times,* July 4, 1930, *et supra. New Republic,* Vol. 64, p. 193, and Vol. 65, p. 179.

thing honest, where you get a nice return and all you've got to do is lend your name.

GROCER: I ain't signin' nobody's notes, mister. I got caught that way once before.

POLITICIAN: You don't have to sign anything, Mr. Norris.

GROCER (quickly): How'd you know my name?

POLITICIAN: Oh, I've heard about you. It's George W. Norris, isn't it?

GROCER: That's right, though I'm mighty curious to know how you found it out.

POLITICIAN: I have ways. Now about this proposition of mine. How would you like to become a candidate for the Republican nomination for United States Senator from Nebraska?

GROCER: Me?

POLITICIAN: Certainly! You're as good a man as anyone else for the job and I think you ought to get it.

GROCER: But there is a Senator named George W. Norris!

POLITICIAN: I know that, too. And he's up for renomination this year.

GROCER: But I don't think . . .

POLITICIAN: It might help you over this long hard winter you're expecting, and who knows, you might even be nominated! (*A pause as they regard each other—and then a handclasp, as the lights dim to half.* POLITICIAN *exits right.* GROCER *remains standing.*)

LOUDSPEAKER: In an attempt to confuse the voters the name of this man was placed alongside the real George W. Norris, but the Supreme Court of Nebraska ruled it out!

Blackout

LOUDSPEAKER: It was later revealed that $400,000 had been spent to defeat Senator Norris.

SCENE FOURTEEN
(*Municipal Ownership*)

CHARACTERS

LOUDSPEAKER

MEN ⎱
WOMEN ⎰ Stage left

MEN ⎱
WOMEN ⎰ Stage right

MAYOR CLARE W. H. BANGS, of Huntington, Indiana
SECRETARY to Mayor Bangs
CARL D. THOMPSON, Secretary of Public Ownership League of America
MAN, Federal Trade Commission Spokesman
BERNARD F. WEADOCK, Managing Director, Edison Electric Institute
JOHN E. RANKIN, Democratic Representative from Mississippi
A SECOND CONGRESSMAN
A THIRD CONGRESSMAN

(*Map of the United States is projected.*)

LOUDSPEAKER: Two thousand five hundred and eighty-one municipalities in the United States and Canada with municipally owned power plants claim successful advantages over private ownership.* Some striking examples . . . Cleveland, Ohio.†

(*Lights come up, left of center and right of center.* WOMAN *enters, left, walks to center.*)

WOMAN [*left*]: Private ownership, per kilowatt hour, fifteen cents.

(MAN *enters, right, walks to center. As other* MEN *and*

---

* Public Ownership League of America *Bulletin* No. 40, pp. 1-2.
† *Ibid.*, p. 3.

WOMEN *appear they make a wedge-shaped line across stage, working from center to left and center to right.*)

MAN [*right*]: Municipal ownership per kilowatt hour, three cents.

LOUDSPEAKER: Seattle, Washington . . .

MAN [*left*]: Private ownership, twenty cents.

MAN [*right*]: Municipal ownership, five cents.

LOUDSPEAKER: Springfield, Illinois . . .

WOMAN [*left*]: Private ownership, eleven cents.

MAN [*right*]: Municipal ownership, six cents.

LOUDSPEAKER: Winnipeg, Manitoba, Canada . . .

WOMAN [*left*]: Private ownership, twenty cents.

MAN [*right*]: Municipal ownership, three cents.

LOUDSPEAKER: London, Ontario, Canada . . .

WOMAN [*left*]: Private ownership, nine cents.

MAN [*right*]: Municipal ownership, one and a half cents.

LOUDSPEAKER: January 1st, 1935. . . . Two hours and forty-five minutes after Mayor Clare Bangs takes office as Chief Executive of Huntington, Indiana, the first power from Huntington's municipally owned plant (used since 1885 to light streets, alleys and public buildings) flows into a Huntington citizen's home. This service came one hour and ten minutes ahead of an injunction obtained by the Insull interests. The mayor defies the injunction and goes to jail.*

(*The lights come up on the* MAYOR, *who is in small set jail piece. He is talking through the bars to his* SECRETARY, *who is standing right of jail.*)

SECRETARY: Mr. Mayor, you can't stay here.

MAYOR BANGS: I'll rot here if I have to.

SECRETARY: Fifteen hundred dollars will get you out, and at least a dozen people called up today to put it up.

MAYOR BANGS: Tell them to mind their own business. I'll

* *Public Ownership*, Vol. XVII, No. 6.

stay here and I'll run the city from here. . . . The Corporation Counsel tells me the treasurer has been enjoined from paying any bills for the city's power plant.

SECRETARY: That's right.

MAYOR BANGS: Call a mass meeting in my name and announce for me that I want the citizens of this community to contribute the money to pay the workers.

SECRETARY: Yes, sir!

MAYOR BANGS: Wait a minute. Tell them I'll stay in jail for the rest of my life if it'll beat Insull and give Huntington fair electric rates. (MAYOR *exits, set piece is removed. General lighting comes up covering entire stage.*)

LOUDSPEAKER: Pasadena, California . . .

(*Following additional* MEN *and* WOMEN *join left and right first set, already in line.*)

MAN [*left*]: Private ownership, fifteen cents.

(*Light comes up on* MAN, *right.*)

WOMAN [*right*]: Municipal ownership, five cents.

LOUDSPEAKER: Jamestown, New York . . .

WOMAN [*left*]: Private ownership, ten cents.

MAN [*right*]: Municipal ownership, five cents.

LOUDSPEAKER: Ottawa, Ontario, Canada . . .

WOMAN [*left*]: Private ownership, seven cents.

MAN [*right*]: Municipal ownership, one cent.

LOUDSPEAKER: Carl D. Thompson, Secretary of the Public Ownership League of America, says: *

(THOMPSON *enters and comes down in front of line of people.*)

CARL THOMPSON: Municipal plants invariably reduce rates. The greatest advantage of all lies in the fact that a municipal plant always pays off its capital account—private companies do not.

* Public Ownership League of America *Bulletin* No. 40, pp. 1-2.

LOUDSPEAKER: The Federal Trade Commission found . . .
(MAN *enters and comes up to right of* THOMPSON.)

MAN (*Federal Trade Commission spokesman*): . . . that private utilities' capital accounts had watered stocks to the amount of nine hundred and twenty-five million dollars.*

LOUDSPEAKER: Bernard F. Weadock, managing director of the Edison Electric Institute, wishes to answer that . . .
(WEADOCK *enters, comes up center.*)

WEADOCK: . . . Inaccurate, undependable, unreliable, false theories, innuendoes, insinuations, distorted facts, and academic theories.†

LOUDSPEAKER: Lincoln, Nebraska . . .
(*Following additional* MEN *and* WOMEN *join line right and left, completing the wedge.*)

WOMAN [*left*]: Private ownership, twelve cents.

WOMAN [*right*]: Municipal ownership, five cents.

LOUDSPEAKER: Toronto . . .

MAN [*left*]: Private, eight cents.

MAN [*right*]: Municipal, one and seven-tenths cents.
(*The V-shaped wedge of* MEN *and* WOMEN *moves forward and the others on the stage move to right and left to permit the newcomers to dominate the scene.*)

LOUDSPEAKER: Bulletin—January 21st, 1937: A power bloc consisting of one hundred and sixty members of the House of Representatives is formed in Congress. Representative John E. Rankin, Democrat, Mississippi . . .
(RANKIN *enters from left with two* CONGRESSMEN—*comes left center in front of line. Projection dissolves into a picture of the United States capitol dome.*)

---

* *Findings of Federal Trade Commission*, by Bernard F. Weadock, Edison Electric Institute publication, S. 14.

† *Findings of Federal Trade Commission*, by Bernard F. Weadock, Edison Electric Institute publication, S. 14.

RANKIN: We have formed a bloc in the House of Representatives to save for the American people, now and for all time to come, the hydro-electric power of the nation.*

SECOND CONGRESSMAN: We are opposed to pooling public facilities with private power interests.†

THIRD CONGRESSMAN: We are opposed to selling public power wholesale to private power companies.‡

RANKIN: We favor the municipalities *owning their own distribution systems.*§

(*Lights slowly dim out during the following dialogue.*)

LOUDSPEAKER: Cleveland . . .

WOMAN [*left*]: Private, fifteen cents . . .

MAN [*right*]: Municipal, three . . .

LOUDSPEAKER: Seattle . . .

MAN [*left*]: Private, twenty . . .

MAN [*right*]: Municipal, six.

LOUDSPEAKER: Winnipeg . . .

WOMAN [*left*]: Private, twenty . . .

MAN [*right*]: Municipal, three . . .

LOUDSPEAKER: Pasadena . . .

(*Stage is dark. Front traveler curtains close. Scrim comes down.*)

SCENE FIFTEEN
(*The Tennessee Valley*)

CHARACTERS

Prologue
LOUDSPEAKER

* *New York Times,* January 23, 1937, p. 24, col. 5.
† *Ibid.*
‡ *Ibid.*
§ *Ibid.*

A—Farmer and wife

WIFE   ⎫
FARMER   ⎬ Farm interior

B—City man and wife.

HUSBAND ⎫
WIFE   ⎬ City dwellers

C—Farmer and Electric Company Manager

MANAGER ⎫
FARMER   ⎬ At Electric Company's office

D—City Man and Public Utilities Commissioner

COMMISSIONER
MAN

E—Parade and TVA Song

CLERK   ⎫
PARADERS ⎬ of Senate

PROLOGUE

(Movies of Tennessee Valley come on scrim. They are integrated with the following LOUDSPEAKER *announcements:)*

LOUDSPEAKER: In the Tennessee Valley. . . . Parts of seven States, 40,000 square miles, two million people. All living in a region blighted by the misuse of land, and by the wash of small streams carrying away the fertile topsoil. In these cabins, life has changed but little since some pioneer wagon broke down a century ago, and for them this became the promised land. Occupations—when they exist at all—are primitive, a throwback to an earlier America. Here stand the results of poor land, limited diet, insufficient schooling, inadequate medical care, no plumbing, industry, agriculture or electrification! *(Front*

traveler curtain opens. Light comes up very slowly on
FARMER *and* WIFE, *left, while movies are still on)* Mean-
while, the entire country seeks cheap electric power, and
the demand for a cost yardstick comes from every section.
In the Tennessee Valley, 1933. (*Scrim goes up.*)

SCENE FIFTEEN—A
(*Farmer and Wife*)

(FARMER *seated at cut-out table on which is a lighted
kerosene lamp. He is reading;* WIFE *is kneeling, measur-
ing a knitted sock to his foot, carrying out the action as
seen in the last movie flash.*)

WIFE: * Beats me how you see to read in that light.

FARMER: † What's the matter with it?

WIFE: What's the matter with it? You're squinting down
your nose like you had a bug on the end of it!

FARMER: Same light I been usin' for the last twenty years.

WIFE: Yeah, and look at you now. Them glasses are thick
enough to fry eggs under if we ever got any sun in this
dump!

FARMER (*quietly*): Andy Jackson used a lamp like this, Nora.

WIFE: Then it was just too bad for Andy. Besides, they
didn't have electricity in them days.

FARMER (*folding paper and putting it down*): Maybe I
better read durin' the day.

WIFE: How?

FARMER: What d'you mean, how?

WIFE: How you gonna read when you're out there plowin'
from sunup to dark?

FARMER: Maybe I better quit readin'.

---

* Fictional character.
† *Ibid.*

WIFE: That's right. Don't do nothing about it. Just give in and don't make no fuss, and everybody'll love you.

FARMER: What you want me to do, Nora? The wick's up as high as it'll go.

WIFE: Never mind the wick! How about a couple of nice little electric lights around here?

FARMER: Now, we been all over that before. And there ain't nothin' I can do about it.

WIFE: Ain't there?

FARMER: You heard what Joe Frank said. His farm's bigger'n mine. He can use more lights, and the company told him, nothin' doin'.

WIFE: So, you and Joe are gettin' up a little club to read in the daytime, eh? (*She rises*) Suppose they told you you couldn't have any air, would you stop breathin'?

FARMER: What's that got to do with it?

WIFE: Light's just as important as air.

FARMER: Sure it is, but . . .

WIFE: Don't "but" me! Why don't you go out and do somethin' about it?

FARMER: Nora, if they don't want to string lights out to my farm I can't make 'em. (FARMER *rises*.)

WIFE: Who said you can't? Who says you can't go up there and raise holy blazes until they give 'em to you! Tell 'em you're an American citizen! Tell 'em you're sick and tired of lookin' at fans and heaters and vacuums and dish-washin' machines in catalogues, that you'd like to *use* 'em for a change! Tell 'em . . . (*She stops*) . . . What the hell do you think Andy Jackson you're always talkin' about would do in a case like this! (*As he stands, convinced, she claps his hat on his head, and gives him a push*) Now go on out and tell 'em somethin'!

(FARMER *exits*.)

Blackout

SCENE FIFTEEN—B
(*City Man and Wife*)

LOUDSPEAKER: In nearby Chattanooga.
(*Lights come up on* HUSBAND *and* WIFE. *City dwellers are seated at table on which is an electric lamp. He reads and she peels potatoes.*)

HUSBAND: Well, here it is. First of the month. (*Picks up envelope from table, reads bill, emits a long whistle*) Six ninety-two! Say, what do you do with the juice around here, eat it?

WIFE (*flippantly*): No, darling. We burn it.

HUSBAND: But good Lord, I only pay thirty-five dollars a month rent for this whole house!

WIFE: What's that got to do with it?

HUSBAND: It seems all out of proportion, one-fifth for electricity. If this keeps up I'll have to cut down my life insurance.

WIFE: That'll be nice.

HUSBAND: Of course, if I had the kind of wife who turned the lights off when she walked out of a room I wouldn't have to. (*Rises, stands left of table.*)

WIFE: I did that once and you almost broke your leg going back into it.

HUSBAND: Well, we've got to cut down. Our bills shouldn't be more than three dollars a month.

WIFE: That's what I say.

HUSBAND: Don't say anything, *do* something about it!

WIFE: All right, let's throw out the radio.

HUSBAND: How can I hear any football games if you do that? Let's stop using the vacuum.

WIFE: And me get down on my hands and knees? Not on your life!

HUSBAND: How about the washing machine? You used to send the stuff out.

WIFE: Yeah, and your shirts came back without cuffs. Remember?

HUSBAND: Well, we've got to do something. You got any ideas?

WIFE: I got one.

HUSBAND: What is it?

WIFE: Did it ever occur to you that maybe those electric companies are charging too much?

HUSBAND: Sure it did. But what can I do about it? Bump my head against the wall?

WIFE: No, but you can complain to the State Electric Commission.

HUSBAND: Look, dear. I'm just one little consumer. How can I fight a utility?

WIFE: Tell the Commission. That's what they're there for.

HUSBAND: Why, they won't even listen to me.

WIFE (*rises*): Make 'em. Tell 'em that your taxes are paying their salaries. Tell 'em that that's what they're there for, to regulate things. Tell 'em you're sick and tired of making dividends for somebody else and it's about time the little fellow got a look-in some place. And tell 'em . . . (*She stops*) . . . tell 'em you'll be damned if you'll give up listening to those football games on Saturday afternoon! (*She thrusts hat at him*) Now get goin'! (*He does.*)

Blackout

SCENE FIFTEEN—C
(*Farmer and Electric Company Manager*)

(*Lights come up on desk.* MANAGER *of Electric Company is seated at desk.* FARMER, *left of desk, stands.*)

FARMER: * My God, I've got to have lights, I tell you!

MANAGER: † Certainly, Mr. Parker. You can have all the lights you want. All you've got to do is pay for the cost of poles and wires.

FARMER: But I haven't got four hundred dollars! And my farm's mortgaged up to the hilt already. (*Desperately*) Can't you see? If I could only get juice I could get me an electric churn and make enough money to pay for the poles!

MANAGER: I'm sorry, Mr. Parker, but that's the way we operate. I'm afraid I can't do a thing for you.

FARMER: And I got to go on livin' the rest of my life with a kerosene lamp and a hand churn like my grandfather did when he came here?

MANAGER: Until you can raise the cost of the equipment.

FARMER (*desperately*): Isn't there anybody else I can talk to?

MANAGER: I'm the manager here. There's nobody else.

FARMER: Isn't there any other company I can go to?

MANAGER: We're the only one in this part of the State.

FARMER: Then when you turn me down I'm finished?

MANAGER: That's right. (*A pause.*)

FARMER: By God, the Government ought to do something about this!

Blackout

SCENE FIFTEEN—D
(*City Man and Commissioner*)

(*Lights up on desk.* COMMISSIONER *seated,* MAN *standing, right of desk.*)

---

* Fictional character.
† *Ibid.*

MAN: * Mr. Commissioner, my electric bills are too high!

COMMISSIONER: † Have you had your meter tested?

MAN: Yes, I've had it tested twice. The meter's all right, but the bills are too high just the same.

COMMISSIONER: Mr. Clark, you're not paying one cent more for your electricity than anybody else.

MAN: I know that! That's what the trouble is, we're *all* paying too much!

COMMISSIONER: Mr. Clark, the company that sells you is working on a margin of seven to eight per cent. We consider that a fair profit. And so will you, if you're a business man.

MAN: Look, Mr. Commissioner. I'm not asking you to argue with me on behalf of the utilities. I am a taxpayer! I'm paying your salary! I want you to go and argue with them! What's the Commission for, if it's not to help guys like me?

COMMISSIONER: Mr. Clark, the law permits any private enterprise to make a fair return on its investment.

MAN: It does, eh?

COMMISSIONER: And the law permits any company to charge any rate so long as that fair profit is maintained.

MAN: It does, eh? Well, tell me this: If laws like that are made for utilities, why aren't laws made to help people like me?

(*General lighting on entire stage reveals* FARMER, *his* WIFE, *and* CITY WIFE *in their former positions.*)

FARMER'S WIFE: *And me!*

CITY WIFE: *And me!*

FARMER: *And me!*

Blackout

* Fictional character.
† *Ibid.*

SCENE FIFTEEN—E
(Parade and TVA Song)

LOUDSPEAKER: May 18th, 1933. The United States Government answers.*

(Lights pick up CLERK *of Senate.)*

CLERK *(reads)*: The Tennessee Valley Authority is created for the purpose of: one, flood control of the Tennessee River Basin; two, elimination of soil erosion, and three, the social and economic rehabilitation of the swampland and hill people of this district; four, *the generation and distribution of cheap electric power and the establishment of a cost yardstick. (As the* CLERK *reaches the words "the social and economic rehabilitation" orchestra plays the TVA song very softly. When the* CLERK *reaches the words "cost yardstick" lights fade on him. A motion picture of TVA activities and water flowing over the Norris Dam appears on the scrim, and through the scrim and on projection curtain upstage. A parade of men and women comes on stage behind scrim, singing the TVA song. Many of them carry lanterns. Red, yellow and amber side lights pick up the parade. They circle the stage and continue the song until act curtain falls, which comes down on movie of second large waterfall.)*

THE TVA SONG: †

> My name is William Edwards,
>   I live down Cove Creek Way;
> I'm working on the project
>   They call the TVA.

* *New York Times,* May 19, 1933.
† Used with permission of copyright owner, Jean Thomas.

The Government begun it
  When I was but a child,
And now they are in earnest
  And Tennessee's gone wild.

All up and down the valley
  They heard the glad alarm;
The Government means business—
  It's working like a charm.
Oh, see them boys a-comin',
  Their Government they trust,
Just hear their hammers ringin',
  They'll build that dam or bust!

For things are surely movin',
  Down here in Tennessee;
Good times for all the Valley,
  For Sally and for me.

Curtain

Movie continues on front curtain until end of film.

ACT TWO

NOTE: *During overture of Act Two, a map of TVA territory is projected on house curtain.*

SCENE ONE
(*Small-town Meeting* *)

CHARACTERS

LOUDSPEAKER

CHAIRMAN ⎫

BARBER ⎪

GROCER   ⎬ Meeting of small-town business men

BUTCHER ⎪

TWO SMALL BUSINESS MEN ⎭

LOUDSPEAKER: 1935, Dayton, Tennessee.

(*Light on group, right. Six small-town* BUSINESS MEN *seated on boxes. A grocery store interior is projected.*)

CHAIRMAN (*probably insurance agent*): . . . Now here's the situation: The company's chargin' us five and a half cents. If we get the juice from TVA it'll cost us two and a half or less. Now, what're we goin' to do about it?

BARBER (*in his working clothes*): Seems pretty silly to get me down here to answer a question like that. Let's get it from the Government! (*Stands up and takes step toward center*) So long, boys. I got a fellow in the chair who's waitin' for a shave.

* Fictional characters. Incidents from article by Fred Pasley, News Syndicate, August 20, 1936.

70

CHAIRMAN: Wait a minute, Joe. The Government won't supply us with juice while another company's in here.

GROCER: You mean we got to pay double just because there's a company in here already . . . that if we didn't have light and power, the Government could come in and we'd save fifty per cent?

CHAIRMAN: That's right. But they won't compete with private industry.

BUTCHER: Then the company's still top dog.

CHAIRMAN: That's the way it looks. . . . I had a talk with 'em this morning, and they won't cut rates. Say they're down to the bone now. Cut 'em and they'll show a loss.

BUTCHER: At two and a half cents I could have that electric refrigerator in the store.

GROCER: And I could electrify the whole business—coffee grinder, slicing machine and all.

BARBER: Let's do something about it.

CHAIRMAN: Seems to me there's two things we can do. We can either buy out the plant . . .

BARBER: With what?

CHAIRMAN: I'm coming to that—or we can build our own plant. Lots of other towns have 'em.

GROCER: What'll we use for money?

CHAIRMAN: The Government will lend it to us at three per cent and we can pay it back in twenty-five years out of the profits.

BUTCHER: Will there be any profits?

CHAIRMAN: At two and a half cents we'll make enough each year not only to pay off the debt, but to light every street in town and maybe take care of the pavin' too. (*Excitedly*) Now here's the proposition. (*Stands up*) We go to the company and ask them to cut rates. If they won't cut we offer to buy 'em out. And if . . .

GROCER: And if they won't sell . . .

CHAIRMAN: By God, we'll build our own! (*Slowly, after a pause*) All those in favor?

CHORUS: Aye.

Blackout

SCENE TWO
(*Farmers' Meeting **)

CHARACTERS

FIRST FARMER
SECOND FARMER
THIRD FARMER
FOURTH FARMER
FIFTH FARMER
THREE ADDITIONAL FARMERS

(*Light on farm group, eight* FARMERS *seated, left, on barrels and boxes forming a semi-circle. An old-fashioned stove is projected.*)

FIRST FARMER: . . . Now here's the situation: The folks over to Dayton just built their own power plant. Got the money from the Government. . . . Now just because the company wouldn't put up any poles without we paid for 'em right away, most of us farmers in this here valley are still usin' kerosene lamps.

SECOND FARMER: . . . and hand pumps and churns and everything else.

FIRST FARMER: It wasn't that so much but they wanted us to buy a lot of expensive gadgets and guarantee to use a certain amount of juice. . . . Ain't that right?

VOICES: Right, he's right.

* Fictional characters. Incidents from article by Fred Pasley, News Syndicate, August 20, 1936.

FIRST FARMER: Well, what're we goin' to do about it?

THIRD FARMER: What can we do?

FIRST FARMER: Now you're talkin'. Listen: We'll march right down there into Dayton and ask the TVA to take over the whole county!

FOURTH FARMER: Who's goin' to pay for the poles?

FIRST FARMER: We are.

FIFTH FARMER: Where're we going to git the money?

FIRST FARMER: From the Government! They'll make us a loan. (*A pause*) All those in favor?

CHORUS: Aye!

Light Dims Out

SCENE THREE
(*Directors' Meeting*)

CHARACTERS

CHAIRMAN
FIRST DIRECTOR
SECOND DIRECTOR
THIRD DIRECTOR   Board of Directors of an Electric Company
FOURTH DIRECTOR
FIFTH DIRECTOR
SIXTH DIRECTOR

(*Light on* DIRECTORS. *Six* DIRECTORS *are seated back of long cut-out desk, right.* CHAIRMAN *paces back and forth in front of desk. The others follow him with their eyes, much as spectators at a tennis match follow the ball. An atmosphere of tenseness prevails. The projection is the interior of a board-room.*)

CHAIRMAN (*finally stops and swings around to* DIRECTORS): Well, gentlemen, have you nothing to suggest? Hasn't anybody got an idea? (*They just look at him helplessly*)

This company of ours is one of the soundest in the country. It took years to do that, gentlemen. It didn't happen over night. (*Intently*) Do you know that Knoxville and Chattanooga have applied to the Government for service? Do you know that municipal plants are being built every day in our territory? *Do you know that the Government is driving us out of business?*

FIRST DIRECTOR: We've taken it to the Courts, Sam.

CHAIRMAN: It's not enough. Suppose we lose. I tell you, it's a different kind of fight we've got to make. This is dog eat dog!

SECOND DIRECTOR: We can't buck the Government, Sam.

CHAIRMAN: We don't have to buck 'em. We can stop 'em another way. (*He pauses, then slowly:*) Gentlemen, I hereby suggest a good stiff cut in rates—maybe forty per cent. (*They all jump up, excitedly.*)

SECOND DIRECTOR: We can't do that!

THIRD DIRECTOR: What about our stockholders!

FOURTH DIRECTOR: What about our dividends!

FIFTH DIRECTOR: What about our investment!

SIXTH DIRECTOR: The boys are right, Sam. We're losing ground every day. Our figures are way down. But if we cut forty per cent off, they'll only be three-fifths of what they are now!

ALL: He's right! We can't do it! Suicide, that's what it is!

CHAIRMAN: Just a moment, gentlemen. I do not propose to cut rates and let it go at that. We've got to do more than that. *We've got to get new customers!* * And we've got to make the old ones use more juice!

SIXTH DIRECTOR: Where'll we get these new customers?

CHAIRMAN: On the farms. In the towns. We've got to open up the whole valley! (*He leans forward*) Not only will

* ". . . by November, 1933, TVA was ready to begin construction. It was right then that the Tennessee Electric Power Company developed overnight interest in the district it had neglected for 20 years."—*New York Daily News*, August 20, 1936.

this help business, but it will establish a right of way, a franchise. The Government won't run lines parallel to anybody else's. *If we get in there first, that farm is ours!* Do I make myself clear? (*A pause as they all look at him*) All those in favor?

CHORUS: Aye!

Blackout

SCENE FOUR
(*Competition*)

CHARACTERS

LOUDSPEAKER

A—Rhea County, Tennessee

FARMER
FIRST LINESMAN   } Farm interior
SECOND LINESMAN

B—Catoosa County, Georgia

OLD WOMAN   } Farm interior
VOICE

C—Franklin County, Tennessee

COLORED FARMER
FIRST LINESMAN   } Company agents } Farm interior
SECOND LINESMAN

D—Catoosa County, Georgia—Residents

FIRST MAN
SECOND MAN
THIRD MAN
FIRST VOICE
SECOND VOICE   } Exterior, electric poles
THIRD VOICE
FOURTH VOICE
OTHER VOICES

A—RHEA COUNTY, TENNESSEE *

LOUDSPEAKER: The company acts. . . . Rhea County, Tennessee.

(*Light on farm interior, left, same as used in Act One, Scene Fifteen—A. Table, chair, kerosene lamp.* FARMER *is seated. Enter two* LINESMEN. *They carry wire, tools, etc.*)

FIRST LINESMAN: Well, here we are. I guess you won't be needin' that any more. (*Points to lamp.*)

FARMER: Who're you?

FIRST LINESMAN: Come to give you some juice. Puttin' it in all the farms around here.

FARMER: Well, you ain't puttin' it in mine till you tell me where you're from an' who sent you! (*Suspiciously*) You Government men?

FIRST LINESMAN: Well, not exactly, mister. But we got your application right here.

FARMER: Let's see it.

FIRST LINESMAN: Show it to him, Bud.

SECOND LINESMAN (*Searches pockets*): Kinder reckon maybe I left it in the office.

FARMER: You did, eh? (*Sees tag on coil of wire*) What's this? (*Reads*) "Tennessee Electric Power Company" . . . So that's what it is! Five years ago when I went down there and got down on my knees beggin' 'em for lights they wouldn't give 'em to me. Now they're tryin' to sneak 'em in on me! . . . Well, you go back there and tell 'em now I don't want it! The Government's takin' care of me now! *The United States Government!* D'you hear that! Now go on and git! Go on, before I sick the dog on you! Git! (*Two* LINESMEN *start to exit.*)

Blackout

* Fictional characters. Incidents from article by Fred Pasley, News Syndicate, August 20, 1936.

B—CATOOSA COUNTY, GEORGIA

LOUDSPEAKER: Catoosa County, Georgia.

(*Light on an* OLD WOMAN *sitting in a rocker. The projection represents a kitchen-stove. Suddenly she stops, hearing something outside. She listens. She hears it again. She goes and looks off right and picks up shotgun.*)

OLD LADY: Who's that up in that tree? (*No answer*) If you wait till after I shoot, maybe it'll be too late!

A VOICE: Hey, put that gun down!

OLD LADY: I thought I heard yer! Watcha doin' up there?

VOICE: Just stringin' up some wire.

OLD LADY: In the middle of the night! Who're yer from?

VOICE: Georgia Light and Power Company.

OLD LADY: Company man, eh? (*Points gun off stage and shoots.*)

VOICE: *Hey, I'm comin' down!*

OLD LADY: I know you are. Ye're comin' down fast too! (*Fires one more shot.*)

VOICE: Hey, *I'm down!*

OLD LADY: I know, I can see yer. Now, git! (*Crosses back to chair as footsteps are heard running off. Sits. There is a pause*) Maybe I should have let him have it!

Blackout

C—FRANKLIN COUNTY, TENNESSEE

LOUDSPEAKER: Franklin County, Tennessee.

(*Light on projection of another farm interior. Table and two chairs down left.* NEGRO FARMER *seated at table with two* LINESMEN *at his side.*)

FIRST LINESMAN: Well, Uncle, we're goin' to give you some light around here.

COLORED MAN: What company you from?

FIRST LINESMAN: Tennessee Electric.

COLORED MAN: But I'se already signed up with TVA.

SECOND LINESMAN: That's all right, Uncle. It's all one now.

COLORED MAN: How kin it all be one? TVA's the Gov'ment. You're from the company.

FIRST LINESMAN: Well, here's how it is. You see, the Tennessee Electric's bought out the TVA. Yes, sir, they ain't comin' to this part of the State. So they turned over your application to us.

COLORED MAN: You white folks wouldn't fool an old colored man, now?

SECOND LINESMAN: It's the truth, Uncle. We wouldn't lie to you. Now all you got to do is sign this agreement.

COLORED MAN: But I done signed one already.

FIRST LINESMAN: You got to sign a new one since we took over the TVA.

COLORED MAN (*Putting on his glasses*): Guess it's all right. Guess you wouldn't fool an old man like me. . . . Where do I sign?

SECOND LINESMAN: Right there.

(*He signs.* MEN *exchange glances over his head. Glass curtain comes down.*)

Lights dim out.

D—CATOOSA COUNTY, GEORGIA

LOUDSPEAKER: Catoosa County, Georgia.

(*Front curtain opens. Three* MEN *in front of glass curtain. Only light in this scene comes from front—midnight blue.*)

FIRST MAN (*tensely, to* LINESMEN, *off stage*): Come on, step on it! Don't take all night.

SECOND MAN: Do you want 'em to walk in on us? Hurry up!

MAN (*off stage*): Let's have it!

FIRST MAN (*throws coil of wire up to man on pole*): This is the last! Get it up and let's git.

THIRD MAN (*lookout*): *Here they come!*

FIRST MAN (*to* MEN, *off stage*): *Here they come!* Beat it! (*Three* MEN *run across stage and exit. Blue lights from front dim out. Light comes up back of glass curtain, revealing in shadowgraph, electric poles and wires on glass curtain. Two or three* MEN *run on. They too are revealed in shadow.*)

FIRST VOICE (*excitedly*): Hey, Tom, Joe, everybody! They've been here! The company's been here! They got wires and poles up in back of the house!

SECOND VOICE: Get the hatchets, everybody!

THIRD VOICE: Down with the poles! Then we'll short-circuit the wires!

FIRST VOICE: Will they burn!

THIRD VOICE: They'll burn! (*Runs on with hatchets.*)

FOURTH VOICE: Here they are.

SECOND VOICE: O.K. Everybody ready?

VOICES: Ready! Let her go! (*Ad lib, "Look out"—"Get out of the way." The hatchets ring out as they chop at one of the poles. As the pole falls front, curtain closes.*)

Blackout

SCENE FIVE
(*1934: Coffin Award*)

CHARACTERS

CONSUMER

LOUDSPEAKER

WENDELL L. WILLKIE, President, Commonwealth and Southern Corporation

REPORTERS

FRANK W. SMITH, Edison Electric Institute

UTILITIES EXECUTIVE

(Enter CONSUMER *from right. He carries a traveling bag, and crosses very briskly.)*

LOUDSPEAKER: Hello! What are you doing in this part of the country?

CONSUMER: Oh, I just came down to find out a few things about this TVA business. *(Puts down his bag)* Is it true that the TVA sells electricity for three cents a kilowatt hour?

LOUDSPEAKER: Well, not exactly. They sell it wholesale to municipal plants on condition that these plants retail it for three cents.*

CONSUMER: And they won't let 'em charge any more?

LOUDSPEAKER: They won't let 'em charge any more!

CONSUMER *(a rhapsodic smile on his face)*: Three cents! *(There is a pause)* How about the companies around here? They doing anything about it?

LOUDSPEAKER: They've cut rates till some of them are almost as low as the Government's.

CONSUMER: Then they must be losing money!

LOUDSPEAKER: Maybe they are. Let's ask Wendell L. Willkie, President of the Commonwealth and Southern Corporation.

(Light comes up on WILLKIE *and two* REPORTERS. *The latter are taking notes.)*

WILLKIE: If the policy now pursued by the TVA is not reversed by its superiors in Washington—or not restrained by the Courts—the destruction of the utilities in that area is inevitable. . . . No more cruel jest could be practiced on the security holders than to be propagandizing the country with the statement that they—the TVA—have helped the power companies in that area! †

LOUDSPEAKER: Atlantic City, New Jersey, June 5th, 1935 . . .

* Pamphlet, U. S. Government Printing Office, "TVA Electricity Rates—A Statement of Facts."
† *New York World-Telegram,* August 28, 1936.

(Lights come up on FRANK W. SMITH, *center. The projection is a cartoon representation of a medal)* Frank W. Smith, Chairman of the Prize Awards Committee of the Edison Electric Institute.

SMITH: For accomplishing one of the most remarkable increases in residential, commercial and industrial power sales in the history of this great industry, the Charles Coffin award for outstanding accomplishments during the year 1934 is hereby awarded to the Tennessee Electric Power Company.*

LOUDSPEAKER: The Tennessee Electric Power Company is owned by the Commonwealth and Southern Corporation. The President of the Commonwealth and Southern Corporation is Wendell L. Willkie.

(WILLKIE *and* SMITH *make low bows to each other. Blackout on everything except front spot on* CONSUMER. *Front curtain closes back of him.)*

CONSUMER: I don't get this. I don't get this at all.

LOUDSPEAKER: What's on your mind now?

CONSUMER: If the electric companies down here are showing the biggest increases in their history, what are they complaining about?

LOUDSPEAKER: They claim the Government has no right to go into the power business.

CONSUMER: Even if it does the company good and their stocks go up?

LOUDSPEAKER: Even if it does the comp—

(Light comes up on UTILITIES EXECUTIVE, *right.)*

EXECUTIVE *(interrupting)*: That's not the point! We object because it's interfering with private initiative, competing with private industry—and it's not *the American way!* Furthermore, *it's unconstitutional* . . .

Blackout

* Fred Pasley's Article No. 4, *Daily News,* August 23, 1936.

SCENE SIX
(*Finale—TVA*)

CHARACTERS

TWO MEN ON STREET
MAN ON SOAP BOX
BROKER (MAN)
STOCKHOLDER (WOMAN)
DISTRICT COURT JUDGE
FIRST BUSINESS MAN
SECOND MAN
SECOND BUSINESS MAN
HOUSEWIFE
SECOND HOUSEWIFE
COURT OF APPEALS JUDGE
CROWD OF MEN
FARMER
WORKER

} Pairs of characters for and against TVA

LOUDSPEAKER
VOICE OF CHIEF JUSTICE HUGHES
FORNEY JOHNSTON } Counsel for
JAMES M. BECK } Stockholders
VOICE OF JUSTICE MC REYNOLDS
JOHN LORD O'BRIAN, Counsel for Gov't.

} Supreme Court

FARMER
ELECTRIC SERVICE COMMISSIONER
CITY MANAGER
PUBLIC SERVICE COMMISSIONER

} Flash-backs of previous scenes

FARMER
BUSINESS MAN
CITY DWELLER
CONSUMER-AT-LARGE

} The public

MAN
GOVERNOR BIBB GRAVES, of Alabama
GOVERNOR HILL MC ALISTER, of Tennessee
SENATOR GEORGE W. NORRIS, of Nebraska
PARADERS
    FIRST MAN
    SECOND MAN
    FIRST WOMAN
    SECOND WOMAN
    THIRD MAN
    THIRD WOMAN
    FOURTH MAN
    FIFTH MAN
    FOURTH WOMAN
    SIXTH MAN
    FIFTH WOMAN
    SIXTH WOMAN
    SEVENTH MAN
    EIGHTH MAN
    NINTH MAN
ANOTHER MAN
JAMES LAWRENCE FLY, Solicitor
REPRESENTATIVE JOHN E. RANKIN, Mississippi
OTHER PARADERS

} TVA

(*Lights come up on two* MEN *walking across stage, left to right. As these* MEN *cross stage, lights hit various groups one after another, showing similar scenes depicting the tremendous interest and argument the TVA question has provoked all over the country. The groups include* MAN ON STREET, EXECUTIVE, MAN ON A SOAP BOX, *a* BROKER *and a* STOCKHOLDER, *two* BUSINESS MEN, JUDGES *rendering the early decisions on TVA. The lines are flung out staccato.*)

MAN ON STREET: What do I care? If it cuts my bills I'm for it!

EXECUTIVE: It's un-American, that's what it is!

STOCKHOLDER [*Woman*]: What about my stocks? What about my dividends?

DISTRICT COURT JUDGE: Unconstitutional!

FIRST BUSINESS MAN: This means the death sentence for private industry!

MAN ON SOAP BOX: We've got to have a yardstick!

(*A group of* WORKING MEN *and* WOMEN *straggle in.*)

SECOND BUSINESS MAN: The yardstick is unfair!

MAN ON SOAP BOX: The Government has the right!

SECOND BUSINESS MAN: The Government has *no* right!

MEN (*in* CROWD—*ad libbing*): Un-American; it's fair; it's unfair; unconstitutional; the Government has the right; the Government has no right; constitutional; yes; no!

FARMER: We need light!

WORKER: We need power!

(*The lights dim out slowly. Single words are heard above the music: un-American! Stocks! Dividends! Unconstitutional! Yardstick! Light! Power!, etc., etc. Above this is heard the* LOUDSPEAKER.)

LOUDSPEAKER: The argument grows! East and West, the man on the street, the consumer, the stockholder, all take it up! The lower court says:

(*Light on* JUDGE *on platform, right.*)

DISTRICT COURT JUDGE: Unconstitutional!

LOUDSPEAKER: The Court of Appeals says:

(*Light on* JUDGE *on platform, left.*)

COURT OF APPEALS JUDGE: Constitutional!

(*Lights dim out on* JUDGES.)

LOUDSPEAKER: December 19, 1935, Washington, D. C. The fight to invalidate the TVA reaches the Supreme Court, in the suit brought by minority stockholders of the Alabama Power Company.*

(*Rear curtain opens, disclosing Supreme Court bench, above which are nine masks representing the faces of the nine Supreme Court Judges. Lights come up on the masks.*)

VOICE OF CHIEF JUSTICE HUGHES: Do you challenge the authority of the Government to sell the power?

LOUDSPEAKER: Forney Johnston, counsel for the stockholders.

(*Light on* JOHNSTON *on platform, left center.*)

JOHNSTON: We undoubtedly do, for non-Government purposes.

LOUDSPEAKER: James M. Beck for the stockholders.

(*Light on* BECK *standing on platform, right center.*)

BECK: It is a scheme to peddle electricity to the largest number.

LOUDSPEAKER: Mr. Justice McReynolds.

VOICE OF JUSTICE MC REYNOLDS: Does the Government maintain that it can manufacture electricity at Wilson Dam and sell it in competition with private industry all over the country?

LOUDSPEAKER: John Lord O'Brian, counsel for the Government.

O'BRIAN (O'BRIAN *appears on platform, center*): Shall the power which belongs to the people be wasted?

Blackout

(*Light remains on Supreme Court during the following scenes.*)

LOUDSPEAKER: The minority opinion.

VOICE OF MC REYNOLDS: The record leaves no room for doubt that the primary purpose was to put the Federal Govern-

* *New York Times,* February 18, 1936.

ment into the business of distributing and selling electric power through certain large districts, to expel the power companies which had long serviced them.

LOUDSPEAKER: Which had long serviced them!

(*The following staccato scenes take place down stage. In a sense they are flash-backs showing the plight of farmers not serviced by the companies and small consumers of electricity. Light up on* FARMER *and* ELECTRIC COMPANY MANAGER, *left.*)

FARMER: By God, I've got to have light, I tell you!

MANAGER: You can have all the light you want. All you've got to do is pay for the price of poles and wires.

FARMER: But my farm's mortgaged up to the hilt already!

(MANAGER *just shrugs his shoulders.*)

Blackout

(*Light on* CITY MAN *and* PUBLIC SERVICE COMMISSIONER, *right.*)

MAN: My bills're too high.

PUBLIC SERVICE COMMISSIONER: No higher than anybody else's.

MAN: But they're *all* too high.

(COMMISSIONER *just shrugs his shoulders.*)

Blackout

LOUDSPEAKER: The majority opinion, Chief Justice Hughes.

VOICE OF HUGHES: . . . Water power, the right to convert it into electric energy, and the electric energy thus produced constitute property belonging to the United States. Authority to dispose of property constitutionally acquired by the United States is expressly granted to the Congress by Section Three of Article Four of the Constitution of the United States.*

* *New York Times,* February 18, 1936.

LOUDSPEAKER: The Congress shall have power to dispose of, and make all needful rules and regulations respecting the territory or other property belonging to the United States, and nothing in this Constitution shall be so construed as to prejudice any claims of the United States.*

VOICE OF HUGHES: We come then to the question of the method which has been adopted in disposing of the surplus energy generated at the Wilson Dam. That method, of course, must be an appropriate means of disposition according to the nature of the property, and it must be one adopted in the public interest as distinguished from private or personal ends.

LOUDSPEAKER: In the public interest!

(*Light up on* FARMER, BUSINESS MAN, CITY DWELLER *and* CONSUMER-AT-LARGE, *lined up down stage, left to right.*)

FARMER: We raise the food you eat, millions of us. Are we the public interest?

BUSINESS MAN: There are twelve billion dollars invested in the electric industry.† Are we, the stockholders, the public interest?

CITY DWELLER: There are millions of us city folks who stand to gain if rates are cut. The money saved will buy more food and clothing. Are we the public interest?

CONSUMER-AT-LARGE: If monopoly is necessary we must have a yardstick to do the work of competition and keep rates down. Are we the public interest?

LOUDSPEAKER: *Who is the public interest?*

(*The* MEN *turn toward Supreme Court bench as lights fade out.*)

VOICE OF HUGHES: The question of the constitutional right

---

* Constitution of the United States.

† McCarter, Thomas N., "Memorial to the President of the United States," December 17, 1934.

of the Government to acquire or operate local or urban distribution systems is not involved.

LOUDSPEAKER: The decision!

VOICE OF HUGHES: The pronouncements, policies and program of the Tennessee Valley Authority and its directors did not give rise to a justifiable controversy. . . .

(Lights go out on Supreme Court bench. Rear curtain closes. MAN *rushes upon stage, center.)*

MAN: TVA has won!

(A crowd of people comes on from all entrances as red, blue, yellow and amber side-lights light up entire stage. An impromptu parade is started. They throw streamers and confetti and general carnival spirit prevails. Over the noise is heard:)

LOUDSPEAKER: Governor Bibb Graves of Alabama.

(Lights on platform, up center.)

GOVERNOR GRAVES: It was a great victory for the Government. It will enable America to compete more successfully in world markets! *

(Light on platform goes out.)

LOUDSPEAKER: Senator George W. Norris.

(Light up on NORRIS, *on platform.)*

SENATOR NORRIS: It seems to me that this was the only logical conclusion that unbiased minds could reach.†

(Light out on platform.)

LOUDSPEAKER: Governor Hill McAlister of Tennessee.

(Light on platform.)

GOVERNOR MC ALISTER: This is the first break we've got. As Governor I am gratified at the decision, since it means so much to Tennessee. I have always been a backer of TVA and this ruling settles the whole business.‡

* *New York Times,* February 18, 1936.
† *Ibid.*
‡ *Ibid.*

(Light covering platform goes out. Between the fore-going speeches the paraders continue.)

LOUDSPEAKER: Bulletin—October 13th, 1936. . . . Charging coercion and conspiracy, the West Tennessee Power and Light Company today asks the United States District Court for an injunction to prevent the PWA from granting a loan to the town of Jackson City to construct a distribution system for the handling of TVA power.*

(The paraders, who have come to a stop, regard each other in consternation. Lights slowly dim to half light, and blue side-lights come on from left and right. As following characters speak, they step down front and are picked up by front spotlights.)

FIRST MAN: But the Supreme Court decision—

SECOND MAN: —didn't settle this at all!

FIRST WOMAN: Water power—

SECOND WOMAN: —the right to convert it into electric energy—

THIRD MAN: —and the electric energy thus produced—

THIRD WOMAN: —constitute property—

FOURTH MAN: —belonging to the United States!

FIFTH MAN: Authority to dispose of property—

FOURTH WOMAN: —constitutionally acquired—

SIXTH MAN: —by the United States—

FIFTH WOMAN: —is expressly granted—

SIXTH WOMAN: —to the Congress—

SEVENTH MAN: —Section Three—

SIXTH WOMAN: —Article Four—

EIGHTH MAN: —of the Constitution of the United States!

(MAN *steps out from group.*)

NINTH MAN: Yeah! Listen!

LOUDSPEAKER: December 22nd, 1936. . . . United States District Judge John J. Gore signs a decree restraining the

* *New York Times,* October 14, 1936.

TVA from constructing new transmission lines and sub-stations, and from servicing new power customers.*

(*The people brush the confetti from their clothes, and start walking around slowly, dejectedly. During this action all lights except the blue side-lights dim slowly out.*)

LOUDSPEAKER (*continuing*): Thus nineteen utility companies put a temporary blight on the hopes of the people of the Tennessee Valley. The injunction means immediate dismissal to six hundred and fifty workers in TVA, the paralyzing of an amazing social program†. People awaiting the coming of cheap power must wait longer and longer while lawyers and courts untangle constitutional questions. But the people of the Valley decide to fight. . . .

(*Lights come up on a group of* MEN *and* WOMEN, *center.*)

LOUDSPEAKER (*continuing*): The Central Labor Union of Knoxville, Tennessee, adopts a resolution calling for—

(*Out of the group a* MAN *speaks.*)

MAN: . . . for Judge Gore's impeachment. An inferior Federal Judge has seen fit, for no apparent reason, to decide the Supreme Court was wrong.‡

LOUDSPEAKER: James Lawrence Fly, Solicitor for the TVA . . .

(FLY *steps out from group.*)

FLY: This is a serious blow. An appeal will be taken.§

LOUDSPEAKER: Representative John E. Rankin, Mississippi.

(RANKIN *steps out from group.*)

RANKIN: We must put a stop to these abuses of judicial power.||

* *New York Times,* December 23, 1936.
† *Ibid.*
‡ *Ibid.*
§ *Ibid.*
|| *New York Herald Tribune,* December 18, 1936.

(*The lights dim down to one-fourth. The scrim comes in, and movies of TVA activity are shown.*)

LOUDSPEAKER: Again the question marches toward ultimate decision by the Supreme Court . . . (*Rear traveler curtains open and lights come up on Supreme Court*) . . . of the United States. The fundamental constitutionality of TVA will be decided. Upon it will rest the social and economic welfare of the people of the Tennessee Valley . . . (*Red, yellow, blue and amber side-lights come on to half, covering the entire group standing down stage in front of platform*) . . . and the character of future legislation for Boulder Dam and other projects through which the people seek to control their water power, to save their soil, and to obtain cheap energy. (*All people on stage take one step forward.*)

ENSEMBLE: *What will the Supreme Court do?*

(*A huge question mark is projected on to the scrim as the*

Curtain falls

(*The question mark remains on house curtain until house lights are brought up.*)

Finis

NOTE: *The foregoing finale is subject to change when the TVA issue is finally decided by the United States Supreme Court.*

SPIROCHETE

A History

By Arnold Sundgaard

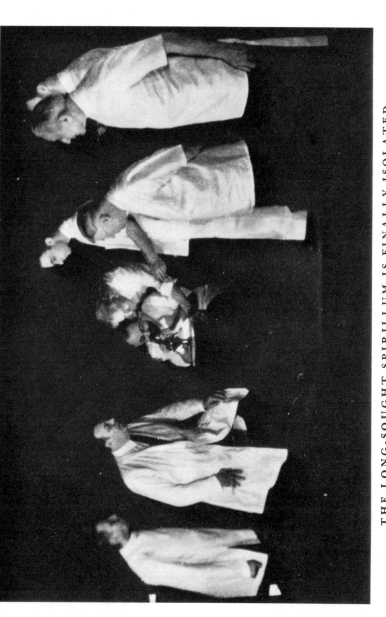

THE LONG-SOUGHT SPIRILLUM IS FINALLY ISOLATED

Federal Theatre Photo by Charles Stewart, Jr.

Spirochete was first produced at the Blackstone Theatre, Chicago, Ill., on April 29, 1938, with the following cast:

PROLOGUE

SCENE—*The Marriage License Bureau, Chicago, Ill.*

(The Year of Our Lord 1938)

Lenny Thompson (A Radio Announcer)	Leslie Spears
Frieda Schmidt	Mildred Kosar
Peter Matzenaur	Thomas McDermott
The Clerk	Leon Edgar Beach

ACT ONE

SCENE ONE—*The Waterfront—Palos, Spain*

(The Year of Our Lord, 1493)

The Physician	Charles Gordinier
Captain Christopher Columbus	Hubert Stumpf

SCENE TWO—*The Tap-Room of a Tavern Inn, Naples*

(The Year of Our Lord, 1496)

Gaston	James Diehl
Pierre	William Ludke
Emile	Stuart Langley
Fritz	Lester Podewell
Marguerite	Barbara Burruss
Rose	Anne Halperin
Loyal	Carl Rodgers
Innkeeper	Burt Maxey
Lucia	Florence Giovangelo

5

Nina   Alice Triantes
Lola   Helen Grossman
First Officer   Herbert Slade
Second Officer   Pat Devlin
Lieutenant   Jack Herman
The Italian   Gilbert Douglas
The Frenchman   Roy Mosher
The Englishman   Charles Conklin
The German   Mark Sullivan
The Turk   Norman Hilyard
The Chinaman   Sabino Rangel
Dancing Girl   Rosemary Shawn

Scene Three—*The Patient's Room*

(The Year of Our Lord, 1510)

The Patient   William Courneen
The Chemist   George Hoskyn
The Sorcerer   Silas Phelps
First Physician   John Allman
Second Physician   William Joy
Third Physician   Albert Storch
Fourth Physician   Carl Adamson
Dr. Girolamo Fracastoro   Elmore Gailey

(The Year of Our Lord, 1600)

The Patient   William Courneen
An Elizabethan Man   Milton Pollock

(The Year of Our Lord, 1665)

The Patient   William Courneen
A Restoration Fop   William Robertson

(The Year of Our Lord, 1760)

The Patient	William Courneen
The Spirit of Girolamo Fracastoro	Elmore Gailey

(The Year of Our Lord, 1767)

The Patient	William Courneen
Dr. John Hunter	Michael J. Kingston
Johnson, his assistant	James Rice

(The Year of Our Lord, 1837)

The Patient	William Courneen
Dr. Phillipe Ricorde	Thomas Brown

SCENE FOUR—*The Office of Dr. Fournier at the Hôpital St. Louis in Paris*

(The Year of Our Lord, 1863)

Jean Louis d'Houbler	Don Koehler
Dr. Alfred Fournier	Charles Lum

The Bride's Dressing Room

(Two weeks later)

Collette, the bride	Margaret Joyce
Marie, a bridesmaid	Carlotta Pacelli
Dr. Alfred Fournier	Charles Lum

Jean Louis' Room

(Immediately following)

Jean Louis d'Houbler	Don Koehler
Collette	Margaret Joyce
Dr. Alfred Fournier	Charles Lum

SCENE FIVE—*Doctor's Consultation Room—Berlin*

(The Year of Our Lord, 1905)

Dr. Hoffman	Alfred Clarke
First Doctor	Grant Foreman
Second Doctor	William Joy
Third Doctor	Milton Pollock
Fourth Doctor	Forrest Smith
Dr. Fritz Schaudinn	Walter Krouse
An Interne	William Robertson
An Interne	Chester Sears

ACT TWO

SCENE ONE—*Laboratory of Dr. Metchnikoff and Dr. Roux
at the Pasteur Institute in Paris*

(The Year of Our Lord, 1906)

Dr. Elie Metchnikoff	George Dayton
The Patient	William Courneen
Paul Maisoneuve	John Connor
Dr. Roux	Hubert Stumpf
The Reformer	Violet Le Claire
Dr. Jules Bordet	Herbert Slade

(The Year of Our Lord, 1907)

The Patient	William Courneen
Dr. Wassermann	Otis Gordinier
Dr. Jules Bordet	Herbert Slade

SCENE TWO

(The Year of Our Lord, 1909)

First Taunter	Myrtle Driscoll
Second Taunter	Hazel Haslam
Third Taunter	Dallas Tyler
Dr. Paul Ehrlich	Mark Sullivan
Dr. S. Hata	Sabino Rangel

SCENE THREE—*A Street*

(The Year of Our Lord, 1933)

First Woman	Belle Hickman
Second Woman	Brenda Brown
Third Woman	Ruth Smythe
Fourth Woman	Elizabeth Rudder
Fifth Woman	Margaret Reeb
Sixth Woman	Patricia O'Hearn

Lower House State Legislature of Illinois

(The Year of Our Lord, 1933)

First Legislator	Walter Krouse
Second Legislator	Glen Beveridge
Third Legislator	Charles Conklin
Fourth Legislator	James Rice
Fifth Legislator	Jack Fleming
Speaker	Alfred Clarke

SCENE FOUR—*Executive Office in a Large Industrial Plant*

(The Year of Our Lord, 1936)

Mr. Thomas	Norman Hilyard
Miss Joslyn	Edna Sexton
John Elson	Charles Healy

SCENE FOUR—A—*John Elson's Home*

(Several hours later)

Mrs. Elson, John's wife	Violet Manning
Tony, his son	John Taaffe
John Elson	Charles Healy

SCENE FOUR—B—*Executive Office in Industrial Plant*

(A month later)

Mr. Thomas	Norman Hilyard
A Doctor	Dennis Wood

SCENE FIVE—*Corridor to the Legislature*

(The Year of Our Lord, 1937)

| Politician | Duke Watson |
| His Clerk | Charles A. Coonf |

Lower House State Legislature of Illinois

(Immediately following)

Legislators—Officials—Guests—Spectators—Politicians

Produced by Harry Minturn

Direction of Addison Pitt   Settings by Clive Rickabaugh

Music by David Sheinfeld

Lighting by Duncan Whiteside and Nat Crawford

Costumes by John Pratt

Musical Program Under the Direction of Edward
Wurtzebach

PROLOGUE

CHARACTERS

THE ANNOUNCER—Lenny Thompson
THE GIRL—Frieda Schmidt
THE BOY—Peter Matzenaur
THE CLERK

Through the years the battle has been much too furious between the eager forces of life and the quick forces of death. In his not unreasonable search for the peace and quiet which he blindly believes will be his without struggle, man has been constantly oppressed by the unseen tyrants within his own flesh. Unknown, even to himself, his body, from the morning of birth to the evening of death, is the scene of a vigorous battle between the something that wants him to live and the something else that wants him to die. In most cases and at most times the something that wants him to live is stronger than the army of microbes and bacteria who would prefer him out of the way. But there have been times when a violent plague or a subtle fever will surround him unawares and leave him begging for truce. Faced with the danger of fresh attacks, man has befriended strange medicines and new sciences to protect him. He has worked unceasingly to guard himself from death. And so in the face of this strong record of achievement it seems incredible, indeed, that he has never seriously challenged the right of syphilis to destroy his body. Because of a confused moral code he has abdicated in favor of this vandal disease. He has accepted its terms without question. But today we are asking: must this continue? Today we are wondering. . . .

All of which is not by way of saying that the curtain is rising and the lights on stage pick out the desk of a marriage license bureau. The orchestral sounds dim to a hum as we hear and then see one of those ubiquitous man-on-the-street radio pitchmen interviewing a young couple about to apply for permission to marry. They are not certain they'll like this quizzing, while they know the clerk waits impatiently at the desk.

THE ANNOUNCER: . . . and so don't forget to get them fresh at your neighborhood grocer and have them on the breakfast table tomorrow morning. Get your order in this very afternoon before his supply is exhausted. And now next on your Anchors Aweigh broadcast is a smiling young couple, who may very well be that boy and girl up the street you've seen holding hands these past few months. They're both very young and they're both very happy. Your name, please?

THE GIRL: Frieda Schmidt.

THE ANNOUNCER: And the boy friend here?

THE BOY: Peter Matzenaur.

THE ANNOUNCER: Well, Frieda, my-I-wish-you-could-see-her-folks, how does it feel to be applying for a marriage license?

THE GIRL: Great! Maybe more girls should do it.

THE ANNOUNCER: How about you, Peter?

THE BOY: I already made down payments on furniture. That ought to show how I feel.

THE ANNOUNCER: Yes, I guess it does. Step-a-little-closer-to-the-microphone-please, how long have you two known each other?

THE BOY: Since we were kids. We lived in the same block all our lives.

THE ANNOUNCER: That's quite a record these days. Tell me, was it love at first sight? I-wish-you-could-see-them-blush-folks! (*They hesitate about replying*) Don't you remember if it was love at first sight or not?

THE GIRL: It couldn't have been. He pulled my hair, tore my new dress, and said I couldn't ride his bike.

THE BOY: She said I had a funny nose the first time she saw me.

THE ANNOUNCER: Would you call it love at second sight, then?

THE BOY: Maybe it was and maybe it wasn't. We just sort of grew up together. We stopped fighting and fell in love the last year of high school.

THE ANNOUNCER: I don't know about this next question. It's—do you think your husband will have any faults?

THE GIRL: I should hope so. I'd hate to marry a perfect man.

THE ANNOUNCER: Really?

THE BOY: I'd hate to marry a perfect wife.

THE ANNOUNCER: In that case you two ought to get along all right.

THE BOY: We will. Come on, Frieda, let's get the license!

THE ANNOUNCER: Thank you, Frieda Schmidt and Peter Matzenaur, and the best of luck to you. There-they-go-folks-I-wish-you-could-see-them. Well, I see my time's about up and we'll return you to our studios where Don Kline has an announcement for you. This is Lenny Thompson saying good-bye from the marriage license bureau and we hope you'll be back with us tomorrow afternoon at this same time. So long, all. (*As he finishes his spiel the* BOY *and the* GIRL *have gone up to the desk and are now speaking to the* CLERK.)

THE CLERK: Where's your medical certificate, please?

THE BOY: Our what?

THE CLERK: Your medical certificate. We can't issue a license until you've both been examined.

THE BOY: We want to get married—not insured.

THE CLERK: You ought to read the marriage law then.

THE BOY: But what's the purpose of such a law?

THE CLERK: You don't know?

THE BOY: No.

THE CLERK: To put it bluntly, it's to check for venereal diseases.

THE BOY: Say, be careful the way you talk. Miss Schmidt and I have known each other all our lives. She's a decent girl and I'm not going to humiliate her by having anybody think otherwise.

THE CLERK: Why should I think otherwise? I'm only quoting a law. Sad as it seems, there are people who don't even suspect they are unfit for marriage. The State protects those who are. It's for your own good.

THE BOY: It ought to take into consideration that there are still a few decent people left in the world.

THE CLERK: This will help enlarge that select circle. You said something about life insurance. You'd be examined for that, wouldn't you?

THE BOY: Yes.

THE CLERK: Well, isn't marriage just as important?

THE BOY: Yes, but the idea of the thing is disgusting. It makes it seem as though we hadn't been decent.

THE CLERK: Decency has nothing to do with it.

THE BOY: Gosh, when two people know each other like Frieda and me—gee, she's just about perfect.

(LENNY, THE ANNOUNCER, *has been listening to this argument and now comes to the desk.*)

THE CLERK: It's one small way of checking up on a disease that's been around for a long time. We can't examine everybody just hit or miss so we examine those we can. And sooner or later most everybody gets married. Isn't that right, Lenny?

THE ANNOUNCER: Say, a minute ago you two kids sounded pretty sensible to me. How come you're so prudish about this?

THE GIRL: We're not prudish. We'd rather not think about it.

THE ANNOUNCER: Aw, come on now, it isn't as bad as all that.

THE CLERK: Lenny can tell you. He studied the subject for broadcast.

THE ANNOUNCER: And some of it was kind of exciting. Nothing like I thought it'd be.

THE BOY: I felt the same way about measles.

THE ANNOUNCER: I mean it. The way it started and how it spread and what men have done about it. Do you mean to tell me you don't know that?

THE BOY: No, and I don't care to.

THE ANNOUNCER: Aw, don't be like that. Let me tell you about it.

THE BOY: What about Frieda? You don't suppose she wants to hear.

THE ANNOUNCER: Why not? How about it, Frieda?

THE GIRL: If Peter will, I will. (PETER *seems angry with her.*)

THE ANNOUNCER: Don't grit your teeth so. Will you, Peter?

THE BOY: To tell you the truth, there are a few things I'd really like to know. . . .

THE ANNOUNCER: How it all began, for instance? How it spread? Well, like everything else there's a difference of opinion about it, but there are a few things that seem pretty certain. It's not as old as you think. Not any older than our country. In fact it was way back in Palos, Spain . . .

(*The lights have already faded on* THE ANNOUNCER *as the other lights settle on the scene of the opening. There is music at the . . .*)

End of the Prologue.

ACT ONE

SCENE ONE

Characters

A VOICE
THE PHYSICIAN
CHRISTOPHER COLUMBUS

The waterfront at Palos, Spain, 1493. The sound of sea waves washing against the pilings of the wharf can be heard in the dark. A few mournful bells are ringing in the distance and there in the dark looms the darker hulk of the Pinta, *made fast to the pier-head. Feeble, uncertain lights glimmer from the portholes.*

A VOICE: The year of our Lord, fourteen ninety three!
(*The sound of a man walking the plank wharf can be heard and a moment later the* PHYSICIAN *enters carrying a candle lantern. He holds the lantern aloft and calls:*)
THE PHYSICIAN: Captain Columbus! Captain Christopher Columbus!
(*A creaking hatch opens and the figure of* COLUMBUS *appears on deck. The opened hatch throws an eerie amber light across his face.*)
COLUMBUS: Who calls Christopher Columbus?
THE PHYSICIAN: I, the Physician!
COLUMBUS: At last.
THE PHYSICIAN: The people fled when they saw your sickly men and sent for me.

16

COLUMBUS: Yes, we are sick here. Sick as no man has ever been sick before.

THE PHYSICIAN: Scurvy most likely. That always comes from long voyages. It's God's way of saying stay home!

COLUMBUS: Scurvy is a mock affliction compared to this foul pox. Their skins are scaled and great sores like leprosy wound their bodies.

THE PHYSICIAN: Maybe it is leprosy.

COLUMBUS: No, it isn't leprosy. I've seen that disease, too, and it's unlike this. This is like all plagues in one.

THE PHYSICIAN: You've met devils in your travels.

COLUMBUS: I agree we met many things. This was the worst.

THE PHYSICIAN: How think you it came?

COLUMBUS: On warm nights there were moons and music my men had never seen nor heard before. In Española the dark has a magic to warm the flesh. Native women with full warm bodies and gracious in the extreme. They welcomed us.

THE PHYSICIAN: So that's how you spent the Queen's money?

COLUMBUS: But they left a mark beyond quick forgetting.

THE PHYSICIAN: A just penalty for sin.

COLUMBUS: A most cruel ungodly penalty.

THE PHYSICIAN: The Queen felt sorry for you and said I should see what I could do. How do you get aboard your pestilential tub?

COLUMBUS: You'll find a gangplank to the left there. Walk carefully or you'll drop into the harbor.

THE PHYSICIAN: I'll be right up. (*The* PHYSICIAN *goes off and can be heard tramping up the squeaky gangplank.* COLUMBUS *stands at the rail looking back across the sea. The music grows with the heaving waves below.*)

COLUMBUS: We sought a passage to the east by sailing west! We fell on lands we'd never mapped before. India maybe and yet not like India. We fought strange new seas with frightened men and this is our reward—frightful sores

such as man has never known before. We find there's
more to discovery than a few new trees, a cheaper spice,
a shorter route. For every tree there's a potential rot;
for every fruit potential worm. (*The* PHYSICIAN *has come
up opposite him.*)

THE PHYSICIAN: I saw one of the sick men on my way up.
It's not a pretty disease; I'll say that for it.

COLUMBUS: Will it last long?

THE PHYSICIAN: The disease or the man?

COLUMBUS: Either one.

THE PHYSICIAN: Oh, those things come and go, you know.
It may be like the locusts that come every seven years.
They go and this may go, too.

COLUMBUS: Seven years is a long time.

THE PHYSICIAN: It may only be the dampness of the sea air.
That's not good for the body, you know.

COLUMBUS: I've sailed all my life and never worried about
damp before.

THE PHYSICIAN: There are those who say disease and plagues
are caused by the position of the stars. Not that I hold
much for that belief.

COLUMBUS: More than astrologers have faith in stars. We
sailed by them and trusted them.

THE PHYSICIAN: Some say it's the sign of the devil!

COLUMBUS: All vague guessing for things the mind can't
account for.

THE PHYSICIAN: For my own part I don't worry about those
things. I take each plague as it comes, collect my fee, and
treat them all alike. A plague is a plague and what's good
for one is amply good for another.

COLUMBUS: I have nineteen men below. Can you save them
or will you give them theories?

THE PHYSICIAN: I'll do my best. And that's all any man can
do. (*The* PHYSICIAN *goes down the hatch.*)

COLUMBUS: Before we sailed they said the ocean dropped

off sharply to hell and dragons waited to claw our ships. This good physician must have believed them. (*He looks down the hatch. There are groans below*) What do you think of them?

THE PHYSICIAN (*below*): They're sick!

COLUMBUS: That's no discovery. I knew that.

THE PHYSICIAN: But such a sickness. There's little I can do for them beyond offering a few herbs, letting some blood, washing their sores. . . .

COLUMBUS: I can do that much myself. . . .

THE PHYSICIAN (*coming on deck*): I can prescribe one other thing.

COLUMBUS: And that is? . . .

THE PHYSICIAN: Don't keep them cooped up on this ship any longer.

COLUMBUS: Yes, I suppose that's best because they're of very little use as sailors.

THE PHYSICIAN: Are most of them from Spain?

COLUMBUS: Some live here, some from Naples, some call Florence home.

THE PHYSICIAN: That's where they should be then, at home. Even if you must pay their passage send them there at once. Poor fellows, I'll wager most of them will feel better when they've seen their own wives again!

(*The music surges higher as the lights . . .*)

Blackout

SCENE TWO

CHARACTERS

LENNY	PIERRE
VOICE	EMILE
GASTON	FRITZ

MARGUERITE	NINA
ROSE	FIRST OFFICER
LOYAL	SECOND OFFICER
INNKEEPER	LIEUTENANT
LUCIA	

(*At once the music breaks through with sharp intensity and then as quickly drops to pianissimo as* LENNY *speaks.*)

LENNY: . . . and that's the way it worked. The sailors brought it home to a few cities in Spain and Italy where it quickly infected a large part of the population. As long as it was isolated in a few cities, however, there was nothing to fear until Charles VIII of France took it into his head to conquer the city of Naples. After a short siege the mercenary soldiers entered the city and there they found quite a surprise awaiting them. . . .

A VOICE: The year of our Lord, 1496.

(*The music continues for a moment and then is wiped away by the crash of wine-tempered laughter. A fragmentary song, a happy passage of string music, a banging of tables and other signals of discordant gayety are heard as the lights rise. These show the cellar of an inn at Naples. The frantic innkeeper and his retinue of serving women—catering to appetites of the flesh and palate— are being jostled and hugged and teased by the victory-drunken celebrants. A few exaggerated lights pick out the private mercenaries of the army who are now augmented by the gayer ladies of the town.*)

GASTON: Victory!

PIERRE: A toast to Naples!

EMILE: What a siege it was.

FRITZ: But what a triumph, too. This is war and the spoils of war. Music! Women! Oh, God, this is what I dreamed of when we stormed the city.

GASTON: God keep Charles of France!

PIERRE: God keep the good women of Naples. Come here, my buxom duck! (*He throws his arm around a girl and drags her into his lap.*)

MARGUERITE: How rough you are. Careful.

PIERRE: Careful, is it? Ah, the war has just begun, my sweet. (*And he kisses her and is so occupied for most of the scene.*)

GASTON: That's what I want. War! Give me more war.

EMILE: Quiet, you dog. They may take you up on it.

GASTON: But I do want more war! I conquered the damn city like anybody else.

ROSE: Why do you want more war, stupid turtle? Don't you like me?

GASTON: Did I say war? I mean wine. I want wine.

ROSE: Why didn't you say so? Here! (*She takes a pitcher of wine to* GASTON. *He opens his mouth like a fish in the noonday sun while she pours it down his eager throat*) There you are, pig!

FRITZ: Ah, such are the fruits of victory. She is a good girl.

ROSE: Fool! (*The wine spills down* GASTON's *neck and he blows it out of his mouth like a spirited whale.* ROSE *laughs and falls into his lap.*)

LOYAL: Quiet, all of you! (*He springs forward to address them.*)

EMILE: Look who's talking.

MARGUERITE: Isn't he beautiful?

GASTON: Ssshhh. I like speeches.

LOYAL: My friends . . .

ROSE: Look, he can talk.

LOYAL: Quiet, I say. My friends, the hour is late and love brings wings to our feet, does it not?

MARGUERITE: What a question.

LOYAL: The hour is late, I say, and we were promised women when we won the war.

EMILE: What of it?

LOYAL: Well, where is mine? She's left me.

INNKEEPER (*pushing a girl toward* LOYAL): Lucia, why are you loafing?

LOYAL: Ah, *ma cherie*, this is what I hoped for. Isn't she lovely? Isn't she dark and flashing? Such eyes! (LOYAL *sweeps* LUCIA *up into his arms and rushes outside with her.*)

LOYAL: Victory! what a sweet war.

GASTON: *Vive la France!*

FRITZ: Why isn't this ass singing for us? (*He forces the* INN-KEEPER *to the front.*)

INNKEEPER: No, no, I am out of voice tonight. My throat, it is hoarse.

EMILE: Sing, you fool, we want a song for tired men.

FRITZ: Make it loud and make it good.

GASTON: *Vive l'Italia.*

(*The accompaniment for the song starts.*)

INNKEEPER: Nina! See that everyone is served!

NINA: *Si, signor!*

INNKEEPER:

> Love rode out on the wind last night,
> But not in the saddle was I.
> Gone is the bliss that I knew last night
> And this is the reason why:
> Forgive me an anguished sigh. . . .
>
> Ahhhh, my love sings only tra la, tra la,
> My love sings only tra lay.
> My love sings only tra la, tra la,
> No matter what song I play.
> Her voice is sweet as the mountain dew,

Her smile is fresh as the ocean breeze,
But when she sings as I ask her to,
Her only words are such as these, tra la
Tra la, tra la, tra la, tra la, tra la, tra la.

(*As the* INNKEEPER *sings his song the lights begin to lower in this area. The revelers join in a chorus of the song as it forms an undertone for the following brief scene.*)

(LOYAL *has gone to another room with* LUCIA. *The lights rise on this room, and* LOYAL *is seen backing away from the girl.*)

LUCIA: Yes, it is so. For your own sake, go!

LOYAL: No!

LUCIA: I tell you, you'll die! We'll all die!

LOYAL: No! I won't believe it.

LUCIA: That's why I didn't go near you. None of them should go near you.

LOYAL: You look so beautiful, *ma cherie.*

LUCIA: But I'm not. I'm ugly inside. I'm all ugly. Go now. Please, go.

(LOYAL *shrinks away from her and then rushes outside.* LUCIA *sits weeping as the lights fade. The song increases and the lights come up again on the tap room.*)

INNKEEPER: . . . my love sings only tra la!

GASTON: Bravo! What a fine song. I shall sing it to my children. (*He turns to kiss* ROSE) Come here, you!

(*The others laugh and as* GASTON *is kissing* ROSE, LOYAL *hurries in very frightened.*)

LOYAL: No, no. Gaston! (*He pulls* GASTON *off.*)

GASTON: Why, you fool, can't you see I'm busy?

LOYAL: No, you can't.

GASTON: What's wrong? (LOYAL *whispers into* GASTON'S *ear and then* GASTON *draws fearfully away from* ROSE) It can't be. Monstrous! Come, my friends. (*They start to go but the others stop them.*)

PIERRE: What is it? What did he say?

FRITZ: Tell us.

GASTON: The pox! The disease is burning in the city. Look! (*With a horrified look he points to all the women and then goes to* ROSE *and rips away her bodice, revealing secondary lesions on her breasts. All* SOLDIERS *begin exit in wild confusion.*)

INNKEEPER: Gentlemen, good soldiers, what is wrong? Have I offended you?

(*Two officers enter to see the men leave.*)

FIRST OFFICER (*to the* INNKEEPER): Where are they going in such a hurry?

INNKEEPER: Good soldiers, come back. There shall be music . . .

SECOND OFFICER: Don't stand there gaping like a sick cow. Give us some wine.

INNKEEPER (*recovering from his distress*): Yes, sir, of course, of course.

(*Just as he is about to serve them, a Lieutenant enters hurriedly.*)

LIEUTENANT: Sirs, I have bad news for you.

(*The girls start to drift out now.*)

FIRST OFFICER: Well, out with it.

LIEUTENANT: The men you saw leave are fleeing the city. From every inn, from every brothel, from every hidden room they flee.

FIRST OFFICER: You're mad. Haven't they been promised furloughs, all of them?

LIEUTENANT: They cry the pox is here. They find the women sick.

SECOND OFFICER (*thinking of himself*): No!

LIEUTENANT: The Spanish disease, they say.

FIRST OFFICER: Command them to stay.

LIEUTENANT: You command them, sir, I'm fleeing myself. (*He salutes curtly and is gone.*)

SECOND OFFICER: They must be mad. They'll never get home till they're paid off. Why, some are all the way from Poland!

(*At this point two things happen. First a large outline map of Europe drops into place upstage. Then thrown as a shadow on the map is the figure of a woman dancing a slow sensual dance. As the lights lower, this silhouette fades and scarlet neon tubes spread like a feverish artery through the map of Europe.*)

FIRST OFFICER: Some from England.

SECOND OFFICER: A few from Hungary!

FIRST OFFICER: Others from Russia!

SECOND OFFICER: From the ends of Europe they have come.

FIRST OFFICER: And now they desert like ungrateful dogs.

SECOND OFFICER: Outrageous!

FIRST OFFICER: Here, more wine! (*He offers the* SECOND OFFICER *wine, but is transfixed by something he sees in the other man's face.*)

SECOND OFFICER: What's wrong?

FIRST OFFICER: You . . .

SECOND OFFICER: Why do you stare at me?

FIRST OFFICER: A sore on your lip. You've got it yourself! (*A clash of music and a shudder runs through the fading shadow of the woman. The* FIRST OFFICER *rushes out while the other slumps in a chair and stares stupidly ahead. The figures of the soldiers as they march past is seen on the glowing screen. And then an* ITALIAN *enters and points to the* OFFICER.)

THE ITALIAN: That man has the Spanish disease.

(*A* FRENCHMAN *enters and points to the* ITALIAN.)

THE FRENCHMAN: Oh, terrible, ze man has ze Italian disease!

(*An* ENGLISHMAN *enters and points to the* FRENCHMAN.)

THE ENGLISHMAN: Keep your distance. I can see you have the French disease.

(*A* GERMAN *enters and points to the* ENGLISHMAN.)

THE GERMAN: Gott im Himmel, but look who has dot English disease!

(*A* TURK *enters and points to the* GERMAN.)

THE TURK: Eating pig is bad enough, but Mohammed should kill you for having the Christian disease!

(*And finally, a little* CHINESE *enters but doesn't point at anybody.*)

THE CHINESE: I'm velly sick and I was never sick before.

(*By now the entire map should be suffused in a red glow with these last figures outlined before it.* LENNY's *voice is heard speaking as the long file of men and women pass before the feverish map.*)

LENNY: . . . and thus in twelve years the disease had circled the globe and wherever white men went this new pox was his most adhesive companion. The doctors were appalled at first and were at a loss as to how to study the problems it presented. But they were surprisingly good scholars and learned many new things about their bewildered patient. . . .

(*The sound of the marching men fades away, is taken up by the music as the lights* . . .)

Fade-Out

SCENE THREE

CHARACTERS

A VOICE	THE CHEMIST
THE PATIENT	THE SORCERER

SPIROCHETE 27

THE FIRST PHYSICIAN	ELIZABETHAN MAN
THE SECOND PHYSICIAN	THE FOP
THE THIRD PHYSICIAN	JOHN HUNTER
THE FOURTH PHYSICIAN	JOHNSON
GIROLAMO FRACASTORO	PHILLIPE RICORDE

(*When the lights come up again the* PATIENT *is seen standing at stage center. On either side of him a* CHEMIST *and a* SORCERER *are waiting to be paid.*)

A VOICE: The year of our Lord, 1510.

THE PATIENT: I'm weary. Headaches. I've been to that man and taken this. I've been to this man and taken that. I've been steamed and scalded and bathed in mud.

THE CHEMIST: My fee, please.

THE PATIENT (*he pays him*): Here you are.

(CHEMIST *exits.*)

THE SORCERER: My fee, please.

THE PATIENT (*he pays him*): There you are. (*The* SORCERER *exits.*) A lot of good they've done. I pay and pay and still I'm aching. I've a fever and sores on my body.

(*The* FIRST PHYSICIAN *enters.*)

THE FIRST PHYSICIAN: You've been listening to quacks. No wonder you're ill.

THE PATIENT: Can you do any better for me?

THE FIRST PHYSICIAN: I make no pretences. I only observe. In you I observe the beginning of neuralgia. A very racking sort of pain.

THE PATIENT: I can feel it already. Shooting through my body.

THE FIRST PHYSICIAN: I told you so.

THE PATIENT: Do something.

THE FIRST PHYSICIAN: I told you I only observe. I won't fool you. I'm helpless. (*The* FIRST PHYSICIAN *stands off to one side looking very important. The* SECOND PHYSICIAN *enters.*)

THE SECOND PHYSICIAN (*speaking to the first one*): Have you seen the patient?

THE FIRST PHYSICIAN: I told him he'd get neuralgic pains.

THE PATIENT: And I did.

THE SECOND PHYSICIAN: There'll be swellings of your throat and your hair will begin to fall out. A new observation.

THE PATIENT: What'll I do?

THE SECOND PHYSICIAN: Lie down. That may help.

THE PATIENT: Oh, my throat! (*He sits on the edge of the bed while the* SECOND PHYSICIAN *stands next to his colleague. The* THIRD PHYSICIAN *enters.*)

THE THIRD PHYSICIAN: I've some good advice for you.

THE PATIENT: I need advice, lots of it.

THE THIRD PHYSICIAN: Don't let anybody else drink out of the same cup with you. Don't kiss anybody or let your children use the same bed.

THE PATIENT: I thought you said you'd help me.

THE THIRD PHYSICIAN: No, I'm just trying to protect your family and friends.

THE PATIENT: I wish somebody would protect me.

(*The* THIRD PHYSICIAN *joins the others. The* FOURTH PHYSICIAN *enters.*)

THE FOURTH PHYSICIAN: I've just observed a new fact about the disease.

THE OTHERS: What is it?

THE FOURTH PHYSICIAN: It can't infect a normal skin. There must be a break of some kind—maybe so small you can't see it.

THE THIRD PHYSICIAN: We must put these facts together in a great body of knowledge.

THE PATIENT: Does that help me?

THE FOURTH PHYSICIAN: In time it may. I'd just go to sleep a while if I were you.

THE PATIENT: Oh, won't somebody do something for me?

I'm tired of being observed. I want to know where it comes from. I want relief.

(*And then* FRACASTORO *enters.* GIROLAMO FRACASTORO *was a great physician of his time, ranking, in his day, along with other men of the period—Fernel, Pare, Massa, Paracelsus.*)

FRACASTORO: I think I can help you, my boy.

THE PATIENT: I think God will bless you if you do. Who are you?

FRACASTORO: I'm Girolamo Fracastoro and I've studied the disease for the past fifteen years. I've studied the things these other men have said about you. And now in the year of our Lord, 1530, I think I've found something to assuage your pain.

THE FIRST PHYSICIAN: Interesting, if true.

THE SECOND PHYSICIAN: We'd like to see you do it.

THE THIRD PHYSICIAN: What do you prescribe?

FRACASTORO: It's mercury, gentlemen. Its density is great and it will penetrate the flesh and drive out the disease. Here, my good man, rub this into your body. (*The* PATIENT *rubs it on his chest.*)

THE PATIENT: My, how soothing.

FRACASTORO: Does it help?

THE PATIENT: Yes, but will it cure me?

FRACASTORO: It will give you relief, I said.

THE PATIENT: I want more than relief. I'm ashamed of my body.

FRACASTORO: You need not be. After all it's an illness like any other.

THE PATIENT: With any other illness I'd either die or get well. This lingers on, torturing me from day to day. It doesn't even have a name.

FRACASTORO: Why, I've been calling it the disease of Syphilis.

THE FOURTH PHYSICIAN: Syphilis? Where'd you get that one?

FRACASTORO: Syphilis was a swineherd, you remember? In my poem, and I do write poetry occasionally, he offended Apollo. Apollo took vengeance and gave him this pox. Syphilis means lover of swine.

THE PATIENT: I don't care for the name. I want to get well.

FRACASTORO: Be patient then. No one doubts but at a given time this disease will return into the clouds of nothingness.

THE PATIENT: And in the meantime it strikes my heart, removes my hair, and leaves me dying a slow bitter death.

FRACASTORO: I say no. Listen to me. That which is most essential to a cure is to surprise the disease at its inception, to strangle it before it has had time to invade the viscera.

THE PATIENT: Isn't it a bit late for that?

FRACASTORO: But for you, you must flee from fogs and wet grounds. Choose for a stay a laughing country with uncovered horizon or a hillside bathed in sun. Guard yourself against laziness and nonchalance in your treatments and allow no truce for the disease.

THE PATIENT: Yes, I'd like that; but will I get well?

FRACASTORO: You must try. These physicians have observed you well. After all the disease is a young one—less than forty years old. New physicians will come to study you and will eventually banish it from the face of the earth. This is only the year of our Lord, 1530, and much will be done yet. (Now FRACASTORO *joins the other great* PHYSICIANS. *The lights fade. A clock strikes in the distance as darkness settles over the stage and the five* PHYSICIANS *move quietly on.*

A cock crows. The lights begin to rise. PATIENT, *alone, at stage center.*)

VOICE: The year of our Lord, 1600.

THE PATIENT: I used too much mercury and it almost killed me.

(*An* ELIZABETHAN MAN *passes. He stops in front of the* PATIENT.)

ELIZABETHAN MAN: God's blood, but you're a vile-looking mess. Why do you clutter up the lane with your cankerous itch? Oddsfish, you should be smoked in hell. (*The* ELIZABETHAN MAN *moves on as the clock strikes again.*)

VOICE: The year of our Lord, 1665.

THE PATIENT: And I feel foul.

(*A* RESTORATION FOP *passes by, daintily waving his lace handkerchief at the* PATIENT.)

THE FOP: You look foul. My dear fellow, if you but realized how ridiculous you are. I know what you've been doing, you naughty boy. Fie on you. It's an amusing little ailment, isn't it? I must tell them at the coffee house about it. How they'll laugh at this. (*And laughing heartily the* FOP *moves on. The* PATIENT *yawns and changes his position. The clock strikes again.*)

VOICE: The year of our Lord, 1760.

THE PATIENT: And nothing happens. Oh, Girolamo Fracastoro!

FRACASTORO (*entering*): Yes, my boy.

THE PATIENT: I thought you said something would happen.

FRACASTORO: I didn't think it would take so long myself. But be of good cheer. I see John Hunter coming down the highways of time. He is a great physician, one of the greatest of all time and his name will be revered in all the world of medicine. Maybe he will have something to say.

(*Lights dim and rise again.*)

VOICE: The year of our Lord, 1767.

(JOHN HUNTER *enters. He is a violent fuming little man.*)

THE PATIENT: John Hunter at last!

HUNTER: And I've plenty to say about you.

THE PATIENT: I've been here for over two hundred years.

HUNTER: Yes, and you're not really sick. All those men have been telling you things. They're stupid old medieval quacks and have fooled you long enough. Let's see what's really wrong with you.

THE PATIENT: But this syphilis is no joke.

HUNTER: Syphilis, bah! It's just another form of gonorrhea and everyone knows that's no great shakes as a disease.

THE PATIENT: It never made me very happy.

HUNTER: I know what I'm talking about. They've even named a chancre for me. But I say most of their talk is tommyrot. They said your children might get it, didn't they?

THE PATIENT: Yes, they advised me to be childless for the time being.

HUNTER: Bosh, that's what it is—sheer bosh. And they said you could get it from cups and kissing games?

THE PATIENT: They warned me about playing games, yes.

HUNTER: That's bosh, too. There's too much false knowledge about the ailment. It's all a part of gonorrhea which we can cure.

THE PATIENT: Why have you been neglecting me then?

HUNTER: I'll show you how harmless it is. But first let's clear the atmosphere of wrong learning. You men get out of here. This is John Hunter speaking. Scat! (*He goes up and chases the five* PHYSICIANS *off stage*) Out with your time-worn ideas. Out with you all, I say. (HUNTER *returns*) Now where was I?

THE PATIENT: You said you'd prove something.

HUNTER: Oh, yes. Well, I will. I'll infect myself with your disease and show you how it functions. Oh, Johnson!

(JOHNSON, *an assistant, enters.*)

JOHNSON: Yes, Dr. Hunter.

HUNTER: Bring me the virus of a gonorrhea infection.

JOHNSON: Yes, sir. (JOHNSON *exits.*)

HUNTER: Now you'll see that this virus is nothing to fear. I'm not afraid because I know I'm right.

(JOHNSON *returns with a dish, needle, several sponges and swabs, etc.*)

JOHNSON: Here you are, sir.

HUNTER: This virus is from a man with the same complaint as yours but in an earlier and more vicious stage. Scarify my arm, Johnson, and rub it in. (*He holds out his arm.*)

JOHNSON: Are you sure, sir?

HUNTER: Go ahead, fool! Do as I bid.

JOHNSON: Yes, sir. (*He goes through the motions of scratching* HUNTER'S *arm and rubbing in some of the germs with the needle.*)

HUNTER: Very good, Johnson. Now we'll watch this disease develop and you'll see it's nothing but gonorrhea, nothing but that.

(*The lights fade on* JOHNSON *and* HUNTER *but remain very bright on the* PATIENT.)

THE PATIENT: Think of that! And I thought I was sick! (*He starts to get up but pains seize his body*) Ooooooh! I am sick. Are you sure you were right, John Hunter?

(*At once there is an orchestral fanfare, the bells ring wildly and the* PATIENT *looks frightened. He speaks very slowly.*)

VOICE: The year of our Lord, 1837.

THE PATIENT: Seventy years later and I'm not any better, John Hunter or no John Hunter. I wonder what's happened to him. Oh, John Hunter! (*He waits for an answer*) Where's John Hunter?

(*From another section of the stage* PHILLIPE RICORDE *enters. The light picks him out as the* PATIENT *calls.*)

RICORDE: John Hunter has gone. He died from that little experiment of his. He was too dogmatic for his own good. He didn't dream that two diseases could be in the same sore. That other man had syphilis and gonorrhea both!

THE PATIENT: Who are you?

RICORDE: I am Phillipe Ricorde from the Hôpital du Midi in Paris. I've been reading what old John Hunter said about you seventy years ago. He was quite a man, John Hunter was, and he did many noble things for medicine but when he talked about you he was woefully wrong. Being wrong is no sin but being believed for a wrong is sad, indeed. Has anybody looked at you lately?

THE PATIENT: Not a soul. And I'm sick, too.

RICORDE: Of course you're sick. You're very, very sick. But be of good cheer. Those first physicians who came to see you were right. The things they observed in you were correct. And isn't it strange that one man like Hunter, because he was a great man, could have twisted the whole thing upside down. (*During this speech* RICORDE *calls back* FRACASTORO *and the other* PHYSICIANS.) We must not forget these men.

THE PATIENT: You know, I was beginning to get discouraged.

RICORDE: Well, we're beginning anew today. Let's hope we don't make too many mistakes. The thing we'd like to find out is what causes the disease. Here in Paris we're working on that angle.

THE PATIENT: You mean you don't know yet?

RICORDE: I'm afraid not.

THE PATIENT: My, think of that. Oh, there must be a cause.

RICORDE: But we haven't found it yet. We do know that syphilis and gonorrhea are not the same thing, though. That's something.

THE PATIENT: Yes, it's better than nothing, but Lord, what I wouldn't give to know what keeps me in this condition.

Blackout

SCENE FOUR

CHARACTERS

JEAN LOUIS	COLLETTE
DR. FOURNIER	MARIE

(*The spotlight rests on* LENNY *for a moment.*)

LENNY: . . . and so one hundred and one years ago the search began all over again. Men like Phillipe Ricorde and his favorite pupil, Dr. Alfred Fournier. Dr. Fournier worked at the Hôpital St. Louis in Paris and was the first to see the effect of syphilis on marriage. He saw how the disease brought on degeneration of the body, too. One day in Paris he tells about a young man who came to him. . . .

(*The lights fade on* LENNY *and come up on the next scene.*)

A VOICE: The year of our Lord, 1863.

(*The office of* DR. ALFRED FOURNIER *at the Hôpital St. Louis in Paris. The time is an afternoon in May, 1863, and the effect of the scene should be a suggestion of that period.*

Seated before DR. FOURNIER *is* JEAN LOUIS, *a young man about town.* JEAN LOUIS *is wearing dark glasses in a pathetic attempt to conceal his identity.*)

JEAN LOUIS: . . . and so you see, Dr. Fournier, that brings me to the present situation. Not only have I been, shall I say indiscreet in my affections, but unfortunate as well.

FOURNIER: A very frequent misfortune, I'm afraid.

JEAN LOUIS: But I assure you I . . .

FOURNIER: Yes, yes, I understand. A very frequent misfortune but, I might add, none the less tragic for all that.

JEAN LOUIS: I suppose I thought it could never happen to me.

FOURNIER: Isn't it strange how we instinctively feel immune to certain things. Death, for instance, we can always imagine for the other fellow but never for ourself. On the other hand, a kiss, a physical contact with a woman, we can imagine for ourself but can never quite picture for the other fellow.

JEAN LOUIS: My death was in a kiss.

FOURNIER: You make it sound much too tragic. You are young.

JEAN LOUIS: Not too young to be insensitive to my predicament and the present inability of medicine to cope with my affliction.

FOURNIER: Won't you please take those ridiculous glasses off. If you want me to treat you I'll have to know who you are.

JEAN LOUIS: Someone may enter the office and recognize me.

FOURNIER: We have many prominent citizens come here. Nothing is ever said about it. Besides, no one will enter the office.

JEAN LOUIS: If you insist. . . . (*He takes off dark glasses.*)

FOURNIER: That's better. And now your name?

JEAN LOUIS: Jean Louis d'Houbler.

FOURNIER: Ah, yes. I've seen the announcements of your wedding. It was to have been quite a social event.

JEAN LOUIS: Unfortunately, the biggest wedding of the season. The date has been set for two weeks from tomorrow.

FOURNIER: That wedding, I'm afraid, will have to be indefinitely postponed.

JEAN LOUIS: Too late for that, doctor. The banns have been read, the trousseau fitted, the invitations are out and, yes, even the reservations made for the bridal suite at Ostend.

FOURNIER: I wish you had been as thoroughgoing in the other phases of your social life.

JEAN LOUIS: That sounds faintly like a lecture on sin.

FOURNIER: Far from it. Laxity of any kind makes its own eloquent lectures. Yours is making a rather bitter one.

JEAN LOUIS: I risked and lost. I don't apologize for losing.

FOURNIER: But like most losers you'd like to squeeze out as easily as you can.

JEAN LOUIS: I'm willing to employ you to do that for me. I'm at your mercy.

FOURNIER (*thundering*): Then I must insist that the marriage be called off.

JEAN LOUIS: I told you it's too late for that.

FOURNIER: And yet you swear you love the girl.

JEAN LOUIS: Dr. Fournier, insane as it sounds and coming at this time I know you won't believe me, but I worship her with all my heart. To me she is all that is beautiful and desirable. She's everything that I'm not and want to be.

FOURNIER: I thought for a moment it was merely a wedding of two prominent families. We French are barbarous that way.

JEAN LOUIS: Yes, I know, but in this case it was love, too. Our families wanted us and we wanted each other. But rather than ask her to feed my physical hunger during that long engagement year I sought less pleasant outlets. I'd rather die, however, than lose her respect.

FOURNIER: I believe you, my boy. What I can't understand is—why do you want to burden her with your calamity?

JEAN LOUIS: What reason can I give for deserting her now? She trusts me implicitly and the shock would drive her mad.

FOURNIER: Which shock? The shock of being left at the altar or the shock of learning you're not a god?

JEAN LOUIS: You don't even try to help me.

FOURNIER: The girl will learn the truth in any event. Wouldn't you prefer that she learned it from you rather than from your body? Why add a further deceit to the one already established?

JEAN LOUIS: I don't have the courage to tell her. I couldn't face her.

FOURNIER: Why can't you go to her now, this very day, tell her your story in all humility and if she loves you as intensely as you say she does, she will understand and forgive. Then return to me and rest at the hospital. Later, if all goes well, this marriage may be possible. And I'm sure she'll wait.

JEAN LOUIS: It's not only she. It's her family. They'd be insulted and refuse to allow a later date.

FOURNIER: Yes, I was afraid of that. Oh, God, why is there such finger-pointing at an illness that's been in every man's family at one time or another.

JEAN LOUIS: You and I can't change the world, doctor.

FOURNIER: We must make our appeal to the family then. Trust to their mercy.

JEAN LOUIS: Trust to theirs and run counter to mine. They'd disown me.

FOURNIER: You don't count on much understanding from anybody, do you?

JEAN LOUIS: In a case like this? No. If I hadn't been caught they might have laughed and said it was my youth. Now? No.

FOURNIER: How would they feel, I wonder, if they knew their narrow prejudices were forcing you to heap a greater wrong on the one already begun?

JEAN LOUIS: This is no time for speculation, doctor. The simple facts are, unless I marry her two weeks from to-morrow, there'll never be a wedding. And I'll be an outcast forever.

FOURNIER: It must not be. I forbid it.

JEAN LOUIS: It's not in your power to forbid. I've come to you for help and you wish to ruin my life even more

than I've already done for myself. You can't do it,
doctor.

FOURNIER: I'm thinking of the one you love. . . .

JEAN LOUIS: But you ask for tolerance in a world that knows
only intolerance. I'm going out to that world now. And
you'll not stop me.

FOURNIER: It's fools like you who breed intolerance!

JEAN LOUIS: In this case, it will have to breed, that's all.
If I had the measles or mumps you might stop me but
I've got something you daren't name and you're helpless.

FOURNIER: Yes, I admit that. But please be reasonable for
her sake.

JEAN LOUIS: It's too late for reason, doctor. It's much too
late for anything as simple as all that!

Blackout

(*In the dark a grotesque version of the "Wedding March"
is played by the orchestra. This breaks off abruptly as
the lights rise on the bedroom of the bride,* COLLETTE.
*She is seated before a vanity dresser trying bravely not to
show her anxiety. She jumps up eagerly when there is
a knock at the door.*)

COLLETTE: Come in. (MARIE, *a bridesmaid, enters*) Oh, it's
you, Marie. Has he not come yet?

MARIE: No, Collette, not yet.

COLLETTE: He must have been hurt. Have they looked in
the hospitals?

MARIE: Servants have been sent to look.

COLLETTE: Oh, Marie, what will I do?

MARIE: You mustn't worry. Jean Louis will come if he has
to go through fire and water.

COLLETTE: Yes, he would go through fire and water for me.
He always said so. But Marie . . .

MARIE: Don't be so frightened, Collette.

COLLETTE: Would he leave me at the altar like this? No, Marie; it's not possible he'd do that.

MARIE: Sit down and rest, Collette. You don't want red eyes for all those guests to see.

COLLETTE: No, no, I mustn't let myself cry. I must be calm. I must look my best for him. He mustn't know I'm worried.

MARIE: You look so beautiful. Your mother's wedding gown and that lovely veil. It should be a beautiful wedding.

COLLETTE: Why doesn't he come? What can be keeping him?

MARIE: I said you mustn't cry. Everything will be all right. Look, let me put some powder on your cheek where you've rubbed it off. Sit still. (*She dabs some powder on* COLLETTE's *cheek*.)

COLLETTE: If Jean Louis should desert me now I'd want to die, Marie. I couldn't face Mama again. What would she tell the guests?

MARIE: Collette, you're going to cry again if you're not careful.

COLLETTE: I don't care. Go away, will you? Please let me alone. I don't want to see anybody. Tell everybody to keep out. (*There is a knock at the door*) Oh, Marie, quick, see who it is! (MARIE *opens the door, admitting* DR. FOURNIER. *Both are astounded to see him*.)

MARIE: Oh, you can't come in here. This is the bride's . . .

FOURNIER: I've come to see the bride.

MARIE: No, please go. She doesn't want company now.

COLLETTE: No, let him in, Marie. Maybe he knows . . .

FOURNIER: Thank you, my child.

(MARIE *closes the door after him*.)

MARIE: Shall I stay now?

COLLETTE: Yes, of course. That is, maybe . . .

FOURNIER: If you'd be so kind as to watch outside the door. Let no one enter. (MARIE *looks frightened*) That's all right, child. There's nothing to fear; I've only come with news of Jean Louis.

COLLETTE: Yes, Jean Louis! He . . .

FOURNIER: . . . is all right, don't fear. (FOURNIER *waits until* MARIE *has gone.*)

COLLETTE: Tell me who you are. I saw Marie thought . . .

FOURNIER: . . . I was a guest? I am a guest, Collette, but an uninvited one.

COLLETTE: You frighten me.

FOURNIER: No need to be. I've come to talk of Jean Louis.

COLLETTE: You say he's all right?

FOURNIER: I'm sure he is.

COLLETTE: Then why isn't he here? Why has he done this to me? The time for the wedding . . .

FOURNIER: . . . is long past. Yes. I know. The guests are leaving.

COLLETTE: No. . . .

FOURNIER: The wedding will not take place today. I want to tell you that quickly. (*He waits for a moment before continuing*) My name is Dr. Fournier.

COLLETTE: Then he has been hurt. I knew it. I knew nothing else would keep him.

FOURNIER: Yes, he has been hurt. But nothing so serious that you can't hurt him more by not understanding.

COLLETTE: Where is he? I must go to him.

FOURNIER: Wait.

COLLETTE: He'll need me. Where was the accident?

FOURNIER: I'm afraid I don't know that. I know only why he isn't here.

COLLETTE: Why don't you tell me? I must know.

FOURNIER: Collette, you love him very deeply, don't you?

COLLETTE: What a foolish question when I stand here trembling for him.

FOURNIER: Anything you might learn about him now can't possibly make any difference to that love, can it?

COLLETTE: Of course not.

FOURNIER: Not even your friends or family or his family can really come between that love, can they?

COLLETTE: Why all these questions?

FOURNIER: Because something else has come between you that your families won't understand. But something that you, I hope, will accept quite sensibly.

COLLETTE: Meaning that . . .

FOURNIER: Two weeks ago Jean Louis came to my office. He told me he had gotten in trouble. It seems he'd met a certain woman. . . .

COLLETTE: Yes. . . .

FOURNIER: A certain woman who allowed him liberties that . . . well, young men are impulsive.

COLLETTE: He loved her?

FOURNIER: No, he loved you, of course. It was one of those things that have been happening since the beginning of time but hurt just as much when they happen to you.

COLLETTE: But if they did not love each other. Men do have mistresses, I know.

FOURNIER: This one left a rather ugly mark on him. A mark he might have carried to you. (*This blow leaves* COLLETTE *speechless. She sinks into the chair as though struck*) He was afraid to tell you. He was afraid of your friends and your families. He couldn't come to you.

COLLETTE: He couldn't come to me . . . he couldn't . . . why couldn't he come to me?

FOURNIER: He didn't want to face you, being less than society expected him to be.

COLLETTE: I suppose sooner or later every woman must learn that her man is not invulnerable. I had not bargained on learning so soon.

FOURNIER: I forbade him to go through with this marriage. This he refused to do, giving wild and foolish reasons.

Ethics forbade me from coming to you, although my heart cried out for you.

COLLETTE: Who stopped him then?

FOURNIER: He must have stopped himself. Brooding over the fact must have shown him what he was doing. Lacking the courage to tell you, he still possessed the courage not to come.

COLLETTE: Poor Jean Louis. Is he terribly ill?

FOURNIER: I don't know the full extent yet. (*And then wisely*) But he'll need plenty of understanding during the days to come. He'll be all alone, I suppose?

COLLETTE: Alone? Why should he be alone?

FOURNIER: His friends will all desert him. His family . . .

COLLETTE: His friends? What about me?

FOURNIER: You? I hadn't thought . . .

COLLETTE: I'm going to him.

FOURNIER: You?

COLLETTE: It's not as if he were dead.

FOURNIER: But your family?

COLLETTE: They were partly the cause. We wanted to be married a year ago but they made us wait. They wanted a big wedding. But if we had had each other this might never have happened.

FOURNIER: You do understand.

COLLETTE: Yes, doctor, we'll find him together. You with your science and I with my love will see him through.

FOURNIER: Brave girl!

COLLETTE: Marie! (MARIE *enters*) Marie, order a carriage at once. At the back door. I'm going to Jean Louis. But the honeymoon is off until . . . (*She looks at* FOURNIER.)

FOURNIER: It may be a long time yet, Collette.

Blackout

(The music continues for a moment in the darkness and then the lights come up on the room of JEAN LOUIS. *He is in a smoking jacket idly reading a newspaper. He gets up, walks about nervously, sits down again. The door slowly opens and* COLLETTE, *in her wedding gown, and* DR. FOURNIER *enter. They stand at the door unobserved and watch* JEAN LOUIS *quietly reading the paper.)*

COLLETTE: Oh, Jean Louis!

(He turns and looks at her curiously, neither surprised nor glad to see her.)

JEAN LOUIS: Collette! So glad you came.

COLLETTE: Why, Jean Louis, what are you doing?

JEAN LOUIS: Nothing important. Did you have something planned?

COLLETTE: How can you say that? I thought you'd be grief-stricken.

JEAN LOUIS: On such a day as this? No, not at all. I've been hiding here away from the family, reading. I see they have freed the Negro slaves in America at last. That Lincoln must be a great man.

COLLETTE: You . . . you were reading the papers?

JEAN LOUIS: And why shouldn't I read the papers?

COLLETTE: No reason at all, but today . . .

JEAN LOUIS *(seeing* DR. FOURNIER *for the first time)*: I see you've somebody with you. Why do you let him stand there?

COLLETTE: Don't you remember Dr. Fournier?

JEAN LOUIS: I don't believe I do. How do you do, doctor. Glad to meet any friends of Collette's. What do you think of the slave problem in America?

FOURNIER: Come here, my boy, we want to talk with you.

JEAN LOUIS: Of course we must talk. Please sit down. Or are you going some place?

COLLETTE: What makes you ask that?

JEAN LOUIS: That dress you're wearing? It looks as though

you were going to a party. It looks lovely on you. Collette's a very pretty girl, don't you think, doctor?

COLLETTE (*shrinking back*): Jean Louis!

JEAN LOUIS: It's a perfect day for a garden party. I've noticed some birds in the poplars across the way. They seemed very gay about something.

FOURNIER: Collette, my dear, shall we sit down? (*She sits and* FOURNIER *turns to* JEAN LOUIS.)

JEAN LOUIS: Sure, let's all sit. (*They all sit down.*)

FOURNIER: Do you remember what day it is?

JEAN LOUIS: Are you asking me?

FOURNIER: Yes.

JEAN LOUIS: Don't you really know?

FOURNIER: I'm asking you.

JEAN LOUIS: I'd say Thursday.

FOURNIER: And what date of the month?

JEAN LOUIS: Why do you ask such funny questions? Doesn't she look lovely in that white gown, doctor?

FOURNIER: Answer me, what date is it?

JEAN LOUIS: I don't know. (*His eyes fall on the newspaper which he grabs quickly. He looks at the date*) There you are. The eighth of June!

FOURNIER: And what were you going to do on the eighth of June?

JEAN LOUIS: Read the papers and . . . (*He stares intently at* COLLETTE) . . . and . . . the eighth of June. Collette! This is our wedding day!

COLLETTE: Had you forgotten?

JEAN LOUIS: Forgotten? My God, yes. Where have I been? This loss of sleep! Your gown. Now I know. Forgive me. What time is it? It's not too late. We can hurry.

COLLETTE: But the doctor said you couldn't.

JEAN LOUIS: Couldn't? Said I couldn't marry my sweet Collette? The man's crazy. Of course I'll marry you.

COLLETTE: He said not yet. Later maybe . . .

JEAN LOUIS: Nothing will stop us!

FOURNIER: Sit down, Jean Louis. (*The boy sits down.*)

JEAN LOUIS (*he looks up at* FOURNIER *and seems to recognize him. He sinks back into the chair*): Oh, now I know who you are. Yes, you said I couldn't. You made me forget. You hypnotized me. I was going to and then . . . you hypnotized me.

FOURNIER: Jean Louis, listen to me.

JEAN LOUIS: Charlatan, that's what you are. Meddling in other people's business. I was going to live my own life my own way and then you came along. Get out of here, will you, get out. If you don't leave this room I'll kill you. You've done enough to ruin my life. (*He reaches into a drawer and takes out a small revolver which he points at the* DOCTOR.)

COLLETTE: He's only trying to help you, Jean Louis. He wants you to get well!

JEAN LOUIS: Then he has told you of my condition.

COLLETTE: Yes, he has told me. But I don't care. I'll wait. I'll wait for you.

FOURNIER: You're being very foolish, my boy. Let's put that gun away and talk it over.

(JEAN LOUIS *stands trembling with the revolver and then breaks down and begins to cry.*)

JEAN LOUIS: Oh, my God, what's become of me. (*The* DOCTOR *is going to take the revolver when* JEAN LOUIS *jumps up again*) No, you don't! You'll take me away. How could I forget. Collette! It's gotten to my brain. I read that it does that, you know. It seeps into your brain. I couldn't stand that, I couldn't . . . (*And then before they realize he turns the gun on himself and shoots. They stand horrified as he slumps to the floor behind the table.*)

COLLETTE: Jean Louis! (*She rushes to him and kneels beside him*) My God, doctor, he's . . . (*She is sobbing.*)

Blackout

SCENE FIVE

CHARACTERS

DR. ERICH HOFFMAN	DR. SCHAUDINN
FIRST DOCTOR	LABORATORY ASSISTANTS
SECOND DOCTOR	

VOICE: The year of our Lord, 1905.
(*The lights rise on a row of chairs placed at different levels. Three* DOCTORS *in white laboratory gowns are seated there listening to a fourth doctor who is* ERICH HOFFMAN.)

HOFFMAN: Gentlemen, it should be increasingly apparent that the virus isolated by Dr. Siegel in 1898 is not the cause of syphilis. And now in the year of our Lord, 1905, we must seek elsewhere for the cause.

FIRST DOCTOR: Dr. Siegel's virus is as good as any other. There are as many causes found for syphilis as there are scientists to look for them. Every time a man peers into his microscope these days he comes up shouting, "Ah, at last I have found it!" It's ridiculous.

HOFFMAN: Would you deny there is a cause?

FIRST DOCTOR: I don't deny anything. I merely say medicine is making a spectacle of itself with all these wild guesses.

HOFFMAN: That would end if the real cause were found.

SECOND DOCTOR: They all say they've the real cause.

HOFFMAN (*turning to the* THIRD DOCTOR): Dr. Schaudinn . . .

SCHAUDINN: Yes, Dr. Hoffman.

HOFFMAN: For several years you've conducted protozoological researches which have been the very model of scholarliness.

SCHAUDINN: Thank you, Dr. Hoffman. I appreciate your tribute but if you are thinking of me in connection with your problem I must decline. I'm much too happy at my own work.

HOFFMAN: But for the sake of humanity . . .

SCHAUDINN: Humanity is an expression used much too loosely these past years. I am interested in humanity, yes, but not at the expense of my own researches which, please remember, I consider valuable in their own small way.

HOFFMAN: Syphilis is becoming an increasing menace. One out of seven . . .

SCHAUDINN: Statistics won't move me. Please.

HOFFMAN: I've already spoken to the German Academy of Science. They are of the same mind.

SCHAUDINN: No, no, you're jesting surely.

FIRST DOCTOR: It's a great honor, Dr. Schaudinn.

SCHAUDINN: A great honor to be ordered about like a janitor?

HOFFMAN: Unfortunately, Dr. Schaudinn, we both are employed by the government medical service. As in the army, transfers can be made. I have yours here for transfer to the division of venereal diseases. (*He presents* SCHAUDINN *with a paper.*)

SCHAUDINN: I don't believe it.

HOFFMAN: It's all there. You may as well resign yourself to the fact.

SCHAUDINN: Was this your idea, Dr. Hoffman?

HOFFMAN: I'll be honored to work with you.

SCHAUDINN: And I thought you were my friend.

HOFFMAN: I'm sure you won't regret it.

SCHAUDINN: Well, you certainly are a smart one, Hoffman. Bossing me around this way.

HOFFMAN: I've all your materials ready. A laboratory of your own and plenty of assistance.

SCHAUDINN: It's all as cut and dried as that. Well, damn it,

I never thought I'd see the day when Fritz Schaudinn would be kicked around like this.

HOFFMAN: You forget the purpose of this. We need you.

SCHAUDINN: Well, if I must I won't waste any time.

HOFFMAN: Science has sought this for four hundred years.

SCHAUDINN: I'll find it in four months.

HOFFMAN: You can begin next month.

SCHAUDINN: Next month? Bah, I'll begin now. Give me a microscope.

HOFFMAN: We have one waiting!

(*Upstage on a raised platform there is now discovered an old table with a brass microscope on it.*)

SCHAUDINN: Hoffman, you old rascal. I should hate you for this. What a demon you are. (SCHAUDINN *now walks up to the microscope as the rest of the stage falls into darkness. All is concentrated on* SCHAUDINN *and that gleaming brass microscope*) This is a good instrument.

HOFFMAN: The very best.

SCHAUDINN: You old rascal, Hoffman. Well, what are you waiting for?

HOFFMAN: What do you wish?

(*The music begins here and increases in intensity as the search begins.*)

SCHAUDINN: Slides! From fresh chancres. New infections. Old infections. All infections. Bring me syphilis!

(*A series of busy* LAB ASSISTANTS *enter now with slides. They go up to the microscope on one side and down the other.*)

HOFFMAN: You are foolish for being so impatient!

SCHAUDINN: I dislike this work. I want to get it over with.

HOFFMAN: Here they come. Call your needs!

SCHAUDINN: New infections, old infections.

HOFFMAN: What do you see?

SCHAUDINN: What do I see, what do I see?

HOFFMAN: Anything new?

SCHAUDINN: Anything old.

HOFFMAN: Anything old.

SCHAUDINN: Hoffman!

HOFFMAN: Yes?

SCHAUDINN: What's that spiral wriggling there?

HOFFMAN: What spiral?

SCHAUDINN: Like a corkscrew without a handle.

HOFFMAN: Spiral? Corkscrew?

SCHAUDINN: You heard me! Look! (HOFFMAN *comes and looks.*)

HOFFMAN: I can't see anything.

SCHAUDINN: Look!

HOFFMAN: Where?

SCHAUDINN: See the red corpuscle in the middle of the field?

HOFFMAN: Yes.

SCHAUDINN: Now toward the eight o'clock position.

HOFFMAN: Yes.

SCHAUDINN: A spiral! A corkscrew!

HOFFMAN: Yes. Fritz, you've found it!

SCHAUDINN: Not so soon. One little spiral is nothing. Bring me more.

(*The* LAB ASSISTANTS *practically dance in with more samples.*)

HOFFMAN: This from a young man. Infection two days.

SCHAUDINN: Ah, there is a spiral—a pale spiral. It looks like nothing—twisting.

HOFFMAN: From a woman. Infection five days.

SCHAUDINN: Again the spiral.

HOFFMAN: From an old man. Infection one day.

SCHAUDINN: And again the little pale spiral. Here on the dark field it is small and pale. The spirochete pallida!
(*The lights begin to fade.*)

HOFFMAN: From an old lady. Infection three days.

SCHAUDINN: Still the spirochete pallida! (*The lights are down now and on the screen at the back a slide has been*

projected showing the spiral-like virus on a dark field)
You see it there, Hoffman? See the little spiral like a
corkscrew without a handle?

HOFFMAN: From a young woman. Infection one day!

SCHAUDINN: We've found it! There it is, Hoffman. I hope
you're satisfied.

(*The lights rise exactly as in the beginning of the scene,
only it is* SCHAUDINN *now who is addressing the men.*)

SCHAUDINN: . . . and so, gentlemen, we have conclusive
proof of the spirochete which is present in every infection of this disease and in no other. I might add that
I'm glad it's been found at last because I can now get
back to my own work while you, gentlemen, continue
the search for the cure.

Curtain

ACT TWO

SCENE ONE

Characters

METCHNIKOFF	THE REFORMER
THE PATIENT	DR. BORDET
PAUL MAISONEUVE	A VOICE
DR. ROUX	DR. WASSERMANN

(With the discovery of the spirochete the search for cures goes forward in the twentieth century—the age of sudden, surprising progress. The extent of the syphilis reign of terror becomes fully apparent. But open fighting is hindered by great barriers of silence and social pressure. While quacks profiteer on a population's fright and ignorance, clear-minded scientists are gagged by prudery and scorn. In spite of this, new questions are asked. New answers are found. Almost imperceptibly the battle becomes more intensive, the field of fighting more widespread. Metchnikoff, Bordet, Wassermann, Ehrlich, Levaditi, Kahn, Wenger—the great names are legion. Each of these death-fighters brings into action a new weapon to fight the disease. And with each passing year the scientist begins to feel that he is wanted, that he is needed; and the cries of the people become louder . . . louder and more clear. . . .

But first we must pause at the laboratory of METCHNIKOFF *and* ROUX *at the Pasteur Institute in Paris. At the rise of the curtain the wild-bearded* METCHNIKOFF *is working at a lab bench, his back to the audience. He is humming some mad tune when there is a knock on the door. He doesn't turn to look.*)

VOICE (*above the knocking*): The year of our Lord, 1906.

METCHNIKOFF: Come in. (*The knock is repeated*) Come in, I say! Must I keep yelling ten times, come in! (*The door opens and that ubiquitous fellow, the* PATIENT, *enters timidly.* METCHNIKOFF *is too busy to turn around*) Sit down, please. I'll be with you in a minute. (*The* PATIENT *waits nervously while* METCHNIKOFF *finishes his song*) What did you say your name was?

THE PATIENT (*dolefully*): I'd rather not give my name. I've got something wrong with me I'd rather not talk about.

METCHNIKOFF (*still not looking*): What's your age, then?

THE PATIENT: About four hundred years in round numbers.

METCHNIKOFF: Answer my question. How old are you?

THE PATIENT: I told you four hundred years.

METCHNIKOFF: Four hundred what? (*Thinking the man crazy* METCHNIKOFF *turns around for the first time*) Oh, so it's you, is it?

THE PATIENT: Yes, Dr. Metchnikoff.

METCHNIKOFF: Did you say there was something wrong with you?

THE PATIENT: All depends how you look at it.

METCHNIKOFF: You must be the one with syphilis.

THE PATIENT: Shhhhhhh, please! We don't discuss those things so loudly nowadays.

METCHNIKOFF: Don't we? Why not?

THE PATIENT: People don't like to think about it, I guess. I can't get anybody to discuss it with me, at least.

METCHNIKOFF: How sad. I'm very sorry.

THE PATIENT: Even in death certificates they won't mention it. If a man dies of—you-know-what—they call it heart trouble or hardening of the arteries or brain softening.

If they can think of another name for it they'll never call it—well, you-know-what.

METCHNIKOFF: You mean syphilis?

THE PATIENT (*quite pained by this indiscretion*): Please! After all . . .

METCHNIKOFF: Well, isn't it syphilis?

THE PATIENT: Yes, but . . .

METCHNIKOFF: Then let's call it by its real name. Now what did you want to know?

THE PATIENT: I want to know what you've done for me.

METCHNIKOFF: Me? Well, Dr. Roux and I have been working on apes.

THE PATIENT: Apes? Do apes have . . . er . . .

METCHNIKOFF: Syphilis is the word. No, man is the only one foolish enough to have it so far. But we—Dr. Roux and I—have found a way to give it to apes.

THE PATIENT: You mean you've actually given an ape this . . . this . . .

METCHNIKOFF: We gave them syphilis.

THE PATIENT: Oh, but if you really knew what it felt like you'd never do that.

METCHNIKOFF: But we couldn't study the course of the disease without them. Now we can watch the course of those germs from the time they start to the very finish. We know exactly what happens.

THE PATIENT: I could have saved you some trouble. I know that, too.

METCHNIKOFF: Could you have told me that it takes a while for syphilis to spread through the body? Could you have developed an ointment that will prevent the infection of syphilis if you apply it soon enough?

THE PATIENT: Have you got an ointment like that?

METCHNIKOFF: We have for apes.

THE PATIENT: For apes? What makes you think it wouldn't work on me?

METCHNIKOFF: It won't work on you. You're too old with the disease. But it might work on somebody who's getting it for the first time.

THE PATIENT: If a person knew what was happening he wouldn't get it. Nobody gets it on purpose. Even I didn't four hundred years ago. It was accidental.

METCHNIKOFF: That's what they all say.

THE PATIENT: Well, it was. I was innocent. But it was spring. One day . . . (*A knock at the door.*)

METCHNIKOFF: Excuse me. Come in.

(*The door opens and* PAUL MAISONEUVE *enters.* PAUL *is young, eager, idealistic.*)

PAUL: If you're busy, Dr. Metchnikoff, I'll gladly . . . (*He turns to go.*)

METCHNIKOFF: No, please come in.

PAUL: Thank you.

METCHNIKOFF: What was your name, please?

PAUL: Paul Maisoneuve.

METCHNIKOFF (*introducing the* PATIENT): Well, I'd like to have you meet an old friend of mine.

PAUL: How do you do?

THE PATIENT: Not very well, sir, thank you.

METCHNIKOFF: Well, young man, what's on your mind?

PAUL: I realize that this is an intrusion, but I'm a medical student at the Faculty of Paris and I've just heard of your work here. This morning I decided to come here on a pilgrimage.

METCHNIKOFF: I'm touched by your tribute in coming but you picked a very poor shrine, I'm afraid.

PAUL: No, no, not at all, Dr. Metchnikoff. I couldn't have picked a more worthy one. When I read of your experimental successes with apes I was thrilled beyond reason. I knew at once this was a great moment and I hurried to you.

METCHNIKOFF: For what purpose! You're not afflicted with this "you-know-what" as my friend calls it, are you?

PAUL: No, that's the point, I'm not. But I'm willing to be. I'm perfectly willing to be. I want you to try the disease on me.

METCHNIKOFF: On you?

PAUL: Yes, on me. You've done it on apes. You must do it on man!

METCHNIKOFF: It was just an experiment. We couldn't risk it on a human.

PAUL: Then who's going to benefit by your great work? Surely not the apes who won't have the disease outside the laboratory anyway.

METCHNIKOFF: But it's more than we dare ask a man to do.

PAUL: Oh, Dr. Metchnikoff, I had a greater faith in you. Surely this must be done for man. It's the next logical step, is it not?

METCHNIKOFF: Yes.

PAUL: Then do it on me, please.

METCHNIKOFF: I couldn't.

PAUL: You must, you must.

METCHNIKOFF: No, my boy, you don't know what it means to suffer this disease.

PAUL: I don't care.

METCHNIKOFF: My friend can tell you what it means.

THE PATIENT: Yes, it's a loathsome illness that seeps into your blood, then spoils your body with ugly sores. In time it will strike at your heart, then your brain, first here, then there, and soon you are gone, a wasted, raving man.

METCHNIKOFF: And that's not a very rosy future for a boy of your hopeful years.

PAUL: That's all the more reason why you must persist in your search for a cure. Others are equally hopeful.

METCHNIKOFF: We can't risk a life for them, though.

PAUL: But it's my life. And what is my life balanced against the millions who might benefit?

METCHNIKOFF: My boy, you have many years before you, years of happiness and good health. As an old man I advise you to treasure your youth while you may. Don't put yourself in the way of death until you have to.

PAUL: What of you? Each day you work with death all about you. It lurks in your test tubes, it hides in your smears, it's ready to seize you the moment you slip with your scalpel, or are careless with your pipettes.

METCHNIKOFF: With me it doesn't matter so much. I'm old anyway.

PAUL: But you've a knowledge that mustn't die with you. Your worth has been proved; mine is yet untested.

METCHNIKOFF: Oh, God, I wish you hadn't come to me.

PAUL: I had to. You needed me to make this more than just another experiment.

METCHNIKOFF: No, I can't do it. I can't. Please go and breathe some fresh air again. Once outside you'll be thankful for your life.

PAUL: You talk as though I'd die.

METCHNIKOFF: Death sometimes isn't so bad. But this disease is more ruthless.

PAUL: I tell you it doesn't matter. What happens to me here and now isn't important. But what other tragedies might be prevented because I've come to you is of great, of vital importance.

METCHNIKOFF: You're a splendid lad; I wish I could use you.

PAUL: If I knew your secret I'd do it myself.

METCHNIKOFF: You are determined, aren't you?

PAUL: With all my heart I am.

METCHNIKOFF: Well, if you must, I'll ask Dr. Roux.

PAUL: Oh, God, thank you.

METCHNIKOFF: Don't raise your hopes. Dr. Roux may think otherwise. (METCHNIKOFF *goes to the door and calls.*)

METCHNIKOFF: Dr. Roux!

PAUL (*to the* PATIENT): He's going to do it.

THE PATIENT: You're a fool for doing this. (*He exits.*)

(DR. ROUX *enters. He is brisk and capable and scientific.*)

ROUX: Yes, Dr. Metchnikoff.

METCHNIKOFF: I'm a little troubled, Dr. Roux. A young man . . . but first let me present him. Dr. Roux, this is Paul Maisoneuve.

ROUX: How do you do?

PAUL (*exuberantly*): I'm glad to meet you, doctor.

ROUX: Yes, you seem very delighted. What's the trouble?

METCHNIKOFF: Well, to make it brief, Paul has such a great admiration for our experiment he wants to try it on himself.

ROUX: I don't understand. Are you diseased?

PAUL: No, I'm not. That's where the experiment comes in.

ROUX: But how can we help you?

METCHNIKOFF: Paul wants us to give it to him as the next logical step.

ROUX: Is he mad?

PAUL: Not at all. Why do you hesitate? I thought you were men.

ROUX: We are. That's why we know the value of a human life.

PAUL: Your apes didn't suffer.

ROUX: You're not an ape.

PAUL: Oh, why must you be begged to do this to me?

METCHNIKOFF: He seems quite insistent, Dr. Roux.

ROUX: Yes, doctor, but what would the world say if we failed? They'd call us savage quacks who sacrificed a man's life.

METCHNIKOFF: I tried to tell him that.

ROUX: Don't you agree with me?

METCHNIKOFF (*weakening slightly*): Yes, I suppose I do. And yet . . .

ROUX: Yes.

METCHNIKOFF: And yet this step must be taken some time.

PAUL: Thank heavens for that.

ROUX: The blame will fall on us in case of failure.

METCHNIKOFF: I'll risk it if you will.

ROUX: Just as you say, doctor.

METCHNIKOFF: I think we ought to.

PAUL: Then it shall be done. Make ready with your needles, Dr. Metchnikoff.

ROUX: We'll be right with you. (ROUX *exits.*)

METCHNIKOFF: I guess you win, my boy.

PAUL: I was examined this morning by two physicians, both members of the academy. Both proclaimed me in perfect health. Here are their sworn statements. (*He gives two certificates to* METCHNIKOFF) They said I do not now have the disease, have never possessed it in the past.

METCHNIKOFF: In perfect health. And you're doing this when you might be out swimming in the sea or climbing a high mountain!

PAUL: How can you deny me the right to this? You tell us younger men to be unceasing in our search for great truths. You tell us to be unselfish in our efforts, devoted in our work; and yet you hesitate the moment we try to demonstrate that devotion. If your words mean anything, if you expect our faith to have a meaning beyond your words, you wouldn't stand there and deny us the chance to share in your discoveries.

(DR. ROUX *returns with a suspension of the disease, a Vidal scarifier, a few towels.*)

ROUX: Here you are, doctor. Fresh material from two of the worst infections in the hospital.

METCHNIKOFF (*to* ROUX): Do you still want to go through with it?

ROUX: From the looks of this young man I see no way out of it, doctor.

METCHNIKOFF: Then sit down, Paul. We must work fast. We've infected our apes on the eyebrow. It seems to be the most sensitive spot.

PAUL: I'm ready.

(PAUL *sits down with back to audience. A white sheet is thrown over his shoulders.*)

METCHNIKOFF: We will make three scratches, much deeper, however, than the lesions in ordinary contact. We'll apply the disease directly to the wound. We will wait one hour. At the end of that time we'll apply the ointment. We hope, and I ask God to be merciful, that it works.

ROUX: There's still time to change your mind.

PAUL: No. Go ahead.

METCHNIKOFF: Then keep your eyes closed, please. (*The* PATIENT *re-enters and watches operation.*) Quiet. There. Another. There. And the last for good measure. There! (*During this* METCHNIKOFF *has partly covered* PAUL *as he uses the applicator. The lights begin to dim down except for a small spotlight on* PAUL'S *face.*)

METCHNIKOFF: We're giving this same infection to three of our apes to make sure the infection is potent.

PAUL: This is a long hour. . . . A long, long hour!

Blackout

VOICE: Eighty-six days later.

(*The clock strikes in the distance and when the lights come up again the stage is empty except for* METCHNIKOFF. *He is seated as he was at the beginning of the scene. There is a knock at the door.*)

METCHNIKOFF: Come in! (*The knock is repeated*) Come in, please! (*The door opens and* PAUL *enters. He is looking very happy.*)

METCHNIKOFF: Paul!

PAUL: Hello, doctor.

METCHNIKOFF: Paul, let me look at you.

PAUL: Yes, take a good look at me, doctor.

METCHNIKOFF: How are you feeling, my boy?

PAUL: Splendid.

METCHNIKOFF: Not even a little—shall we say, tired?

PAUL: I never felt better in my life!

METCHNIKOFF: Think of that. And today is . . .

PAUL: The twenty-fourth. Eighty-six days! Eighty-six days have passed and still no sign of the disease.

METCHNIKOFF: Do you realize what that means, Paul?

PAUL: It means you're a great man, doctor—you and Dr. Roux. It means that calomel ointment will prevent the infection of syphilis at the time of inception.

METCHNIKOFF: A success!

PAUL: It's the first step in conquering the disease, a great preventive measure. And here is my clean bill of health. The same physicians who examined me before, examined me today. (*He reads*) "We, the undersigned, have this day examined Paul Maisoneuve who was, eighty-six days ago, inoculated with the germs of syphilis. We hereby declare he does not now possess nor does he indicate in the past having possessed this infection. It is incredible that he has escaped. We attribute this successful prophylaxis to the calomel ointment developed by Drs. Metchnikoff and Roux of the Pasteur Institute in Paris. . . ." (*As* PAUL *finishes reading, the door swings open and a crusading woman* REFORMER *enters.*)

THE REFORMER: Dr. Metchnikoff!

METCHNIKOFF: At your service, my dear lady.

THE REFORMER: As chairman of the Citizen's Moral Welfare League, I forbid you to make your discovery known to the world!

METCHNIKOFF: Do you really?

THE REFORMER: Syphilis is the penalty for sin! You are about to remove that penalty and plunge the world into an orgy of sinful living. Man will be free to pursue his lustful impulses with no thought of any physical wrath being inflicted on him. Think, Dr. Metchnikoff, what that will mean.

METCHNIKOFF: You are a citizen, you say?

THE REFORMER: Indeed I am.

METCHNIKOFF: And you say that syphilis is the penalty for sin?

THE REFORMER: Indeed it is.

METCHNIKOFF: And it's a horrible ghastly penalty, you'll admit. A more horrible one could never be devised, could it?

THE REFORMER: I could think of none worse.

METCHNIKOFF: Then why in God's name hasn't it put an end to sin?

THE REFORMER: Why, I . . . I . . .

METCHNIKOFF: When all your moral prophylactics have failed to prevent the spread of this disease you wish to suppress a chemical one.

THE REFORMER: That's not the way to look at it.

METCHNIKOFF: Telling people it's sinful hasn't stopped it from striking one out of every ten persons you meet on the street!

THE REFORMER: Yes, but if they wouldn't sin . . .

METCHNIKOFF: If they wouldn't sin! The real sin would be to keep this discovery from the world. The real sin would be withholding a cure when one was available!

THE REFORMER: You must think of people's morals.

METCHNIKOFF: Morals be damned! You think of their morals and I'll think of their illnesses. Now get out of here. Get out of here, I say. I'm giving this cure to the world. It's not an important one, really. It won't help the ones who don't know they have it. It won't prevent

innocent children from being born with it. It won't cure
a man once he's gotten it. But it may prevent a small
amount of misery in the world and neither you nor your
self-righteous committee will stop me from giving it to
those who need it. Good day, dear lady!

(REFORMER *exits.* METCHNIKOFF *turns to* PAUL.)

METCHNIKOFF: Prudish old witch, that's what she is. Did
you hear what she said, Paul? As though there weren't
enough penalties for sin in the world. (*The door opens
again and* METCHNIKOFF *wheels around yelling*) Get out,
I told you. Don't ever come . . . (*And then he notices
that it is not the* REFORMER *who stands in front of him
but sad-eyed little* JULES BORDET. METCHNIKOFF *is overwhelmed with joy at seeing* BORDET *and rushes to hug
him*) Jules! Jules! What on earth . . . ? Ah, Jules, it's
good to see you.

BORDET (*after releasing himself*): What's wrong with you,
Elie? First you yell at me like a madman and then you
hug me.

METCHNIKOFF: I thought you were somebody else.

BORDET: Do you send all your women away like that last
one?

METCHNIKOFF: She was a fool, a stupid fool, Jules. But no
matter, how are you?

BORDET: A little overwhelmed by this splendid welcome.
Otherwise my health, good; my mind, hopeful; my
spirits, bubbling.

METCHNIKOFF: That's excellent, Jules. I'm glad to hear it.
Paul, come here and meet my good friend, Dr. Jules
Bordet.

PAUL: How do you do, Dr. Bordet? I've heard a great deal
about you.

BORDET (*looking questioningly at* METCHNIKOFF): Yes?

PAUL: You once worked here with Dr. Metchnikoff, didn't
you?

BORDET: Worked? Slaved! I slaved under this big Russian bear here. I'm still frightened by him. He's mad, you know.

METCHNIKOFF: Oh, Jules, you don't mean that. Don't believe him, Paul. Jules likes me. He still writes to me, asks questions of his old master.

BORDET: Yes, like that question three years ago. That was a good answer you gave me, Elie.

METCHNIKOFF: I'll never forgive myself for that, Jules. Such stupidity! You know, Paul, if it hadn't been for me Jules would have been an immortal man today.

PAUL: How?

BORDET: Forget it, Elie. I guess your eyesight was bad.

PAUL: May I ask what you're talking about?

BORDET: Let's not mention it.

METCHNIKOFF: No, no, Paul must know what a great man you are. You see, Paul, back in 1903—Jules discovered the pale spirochete of syphilis.

PAUL: I thought Fritz Schaudinn did that last year.

METCHNIKOFF: So he did. But Jules saw it long before that. Only he's afraid to say anything about it. In those days everybody is finding a cause and Jules is afraid he'll be laughed at. So he sends a slide to me, his old master, and asks what I think. I say there is nothing to it and Jules is fool enough to believe me and let the matter drop. Think of that!

PAUL: Oh, how sad.

BORDET: What does it matter? Schaudinn found it anyway. I'm glad he did.

METCHNIKOFF: But to think I cheated you of fame, Jules.

BORDET: I say it doesn't matter now. I've found something else that looks just as important. That's what I came to see you about.

METCHNIKOFF: And what is that?

BORDET: They tell me that you and Dr. Roux have found

an ointment that will prevent syphilis at the time of its infection. Is that right?

METCHNIKOFF: Yes, what do you think of it?

BORDET: I think it's wonderful. I'm glad for you.

METCHNIKOFF: Don't tell me you found that three years ago, too.

BORDET: No, far from it. Both you and Schaudinn have worked on the early stages of the disease. That's important, yes, but what about the man who already has it so badly you can no longer see the spirochete under the microscope? What about it after it's submerged in the blood but still carries on its evil work?

METCHNIKOFF: Ah, there we are helpless. Once it's got past the first stage it's gone. It melts into the system.

BORDET: Well, Elie, that's where I come in. I've got a hunch my test will detect it at those later stages.

METCHNIKOFF: No!

BORDET: Yes!

METCHNIKOFF: Think of that, Paul, think of that. I told you he was a genius. Ah, Jules, you'll be a great man yet.

BORDET: The thing is, I wonder if I could work here for a while. It will be easier than taking you all the way to my regular laboratory in Brussels.

METCHNIKOFF: Let's pretend this is Brussels!

BORDET: Ah, very good, Elie. I feel at home already.

METCHNIKOFF: Anything else?

BORDET: Could you let me take a patient who has had the disease for a little while?

METCHNIKOFF: Let me see. Paul, do you think you could find one?

PAUL: I could try. (PAUL *goes out.*)

BORDET: Now I'll get my syringes ready and my test tubes and retorts and what the writers like to call "chemical paraphernalia." (*And he does busy himself with an assortment of impressive-looking paraphernalia.*)

METCHNIKOFF: Would you like to be left alone?

BORDET: That's up to you, Elie. You can stay or go as you like. This is just an experiment and I'm not saying one way or another that I'm on the right track. But it does look promising.

METCHNIKOFF: Well, if it's just an experiment you'd probably like to have me gone for a while. I ought to be getting back to Paris anyhow.

BORDET: I'll call you if anything good comes of this. Thanks for letting me use the laboratory.

(PAUL *now enters with the* PATIENT, *who apparently must have been waiting outside.*)

PAUL: Look who I've found!

METCHNIKOFF: Ah, my innocent friend.

BORDET: Has he had it a long time?

THE PATIENT: Absolutely.

BORDET: Then you're just the man I need. Sit down.

METCHNIKOFF: Come along, Paul. We're going to let Jules have some peace for a while. Good luck, Jules.

BORDET: Thank you, Elie. See you again.

(METCHNIKOFF *and* PAUL *go.*)

THE PATIENT: Nice fellow, that Metchnikoff.

BORDET: Yes, indeed, I owe a lot to him. Now let me have your arm.

THE PATIENT: Certainly.

BORDET (*getting the syringe ready*): This is a fussy sort of test but the main idea is that I'll take blood from your arm and mix it with four chemical reagents I've prepared which will make it cloudy. If it remains cloudy it'll mean you have the disease.

THE PATIENT: But I already told you I've got the disease.

BORDET: I know you have. But in this other tube I have some of my own blood and I don't have it. I'll test mine the same way. If the test is any good yours will remain cloudy and mine won't.

THE PATIENT: I'm afraid I don't understand it.

BORDET: Well, I don't blame you. It's very complicated and I don't understand some of it myself. Now we'll take our tubes and put them in the incubator here till we count ten. That would be equal to two hours of ordinary time.

THE PATIENT: I'll count. One, two, three, four, five, six, seven, eight, nine, ten.

BORDET: That was a quick two hours. Now let's see what we have. (*He takes the tubes out of the incubator.*)

THE PATIENT: Look!

BORDET: I am.

THE PATIENT: Mine's still cloudy.

BORDET: Indeed it is.

THE PATIENT: And yours isn't. Yours is clear as wine. Man, think of what you've done.

BORDET: Wait a minute. Don't get excited. We've got to check this before it's valid. Here's a third specimen I've saved for that. This is blood from a young man with fresh sores. There are certain laws governing these things and everything has to fit. This will prove if it's right.

THE PATIENT: But you just proved it. . . .

BORDET: No, no, not for certain. We'll soon see. (BORDET *puts the tube in and the* PATIENT *counts rapidly.*)

THE PATIENT: One, two, three, four, five, six, seven, eight, nine, ten! Two hours are up.

BORDET: We'll soon know for certain. (*Takes it out of incubator.*)

THE PATIENT: What's the matter with it? (BORDET *looks sadly at the tube. They wait impatiently but nothing seems to happen.*)

BORDET: No, there must be a mistake. The law I've developed says it should stay cloudy every time. And it doesn't. So the test isn't accurate yet. I'll have to work on it longer.

THE PATIENT: A little inaccuracy won't hurt, will it? Who'll notice the difference?

BORDET: A fine mess if we went around telling people they had syphilis when they didn't and vice versa.

THE PATIENT: Yes, I can see that would be confusing.

BORDET: I'm glad Metchnikoff didn't stay to see this fiasco. I was sure it would work.

THE PATIENT: You're going to keep on trying, aren't you?

BORDET: No, not for a while. I'm tired. I'll publish what little I've done and maybe someone else can puzzle out the answer.

THE PATIENT: Do you mind if I look at the notes?

BORDET: No, go ahead. Amuse yourself any way you want. But please excuse me. I'm a little weary. (BORDET *goes. The* PATIENT *looks at the notes. The lights dim and rise again. The clock strikes.*)

VOICE: The year of our Lord, 1907.

(DR. WASSERMANN *enters.*)

WASSERMANN: Could you tell me where Dr. Bordet is?

THE PATIENT: He's out.

WASSERMANN: I'm Dr. Wassermann from Germany. I've been reading a lot about Dr. Bordet's blood tests. I have an idea I know where he made a mistake. I'd like to discuss it with him. (WASSERMANN *looks at the scientific journal he has been carrying.*)

THE PATIENT: I wish you would. He is rather discouraged. I looked at his notes before and they seemed like Greek to me—all these formulas.

WASSERMANN: No, I'm sure it all makes sense if you study it carefully. However, there's one little mistake here. I can't understand how he happened to miss that.

THE PATIENT: A mistake? Where?

WASSERMANN: Right here on the third experiment. I wonder if he'd mind my trying to fix it up.

THE PATIENT: I'm sure he wouldn't. He's too great a man for that.

WASSERMANN: Then sit down here, will you, please?

THE PATIENT: What're you going to do?

WASSERMANN: Prove that this test is essentially correct. (*He lets some more blood from the* PATIENT's *arm.*) We won't need much. And it won't hurt. There. (*He takes the tube, shakes it up, inserts some serum, etc. Then* DR. BORDET *walks in.*)

BORDET: Dr. Wassermann! I'm glad you've come.

WASSERMANN: Dr. Bordet. I think I know the answer to your experiment.

BORDET: I'd be mighty grateful if you did. The world will be grateful if you can fix it up. (BORDET *goes to another lab bench and starts puttering around.*)

WASSERMANN: Aren't you going to watch?

BORDET: I've got too much work to do. I'll leave that up to you.

THE PATIENT: One, two, three, four, five, six, seven, eight, nine, ten! Two hours are up, Dr. Wassermann. (WASSERMANN *takes the tube from the incubator.*)

WASSERMANN (*holding up several tubes*): Well, I've done it!

BORDET: Does it really work?

WASSERMANN: Of course it works.

BORDET: Then the honor goes to you, doctor. The experiment would have been nothing except for you.

WASSERMANN: No. Together we must share . . .

BORDET: I wouldn't think of it. The Wassermann test for syphilis! It sounds good. I'm proud of you. I hope a lot of people will take it.

WASSERMANN: Come, we must tell the world we now have a way of finding the hidden spirochete.

BORDET: No, doctor, you do that yourself. I'm busy. I've some other experiments here. Now where was I? Let me see. . . . (BORDET *returns to his work and is happily en-*

gaged in that as WASSERMANN, *holding the tube aloft, goes out.*)

THE PATIENT: Bravo, Dr. Wassermann. . . . (*Then he looks back at* BORDET) And God bless you, Dr. Bordet. . . .
(*The* PATIENT *goes.* BORDET *continues working in the laboratory. The lights* . . .)

Dim-Out

SCENE TWO

CHARACTERS

A VOICE	THREE TAUNTERS
PAUL EHRLICH	S. HATA

(*The laboratory of* DR. PAUL EHRLICH *at Frankfort, Germany.*)

LENNY (*in darkness*): . . . and thus twice did Dr. Jules Bordet stand on the brink of immortality . . . once as the discoverer of the spirochete before Schaudinn and once as the discoverer of the blood test before Wassermann. He failed because he wanted to make doubly sure he was right. However, thanks to Bordet and Wassermann there was now a way of testing the disease in its later stages. The next step was to find a cure. Paul Ehrlich was a zealous worker and we find him now at Frankfort, Germany. . . .

VOICE: The year of our Lord, 1909.
(*The lights rise again.* PAUL EHRLICH *and the little Japanese* s. HATA *are busy at the lab bench with brightly colored dyes in test tubes. Beside* EHRLICH *stand the* THREE TAUNTERS. *They sound like old haggling witches.*)

FIRST TAUNTER (*pointing at* EHRLICH): That's Paul Ehrlich and he's mad!

SECOND TAUNTER: That's Paul Ehrlich and he's a failure!

THIRD TAUNTER: For twenty years he's been mad and failing. (*They all laugh uproariously at this but* EHRLICH *and* HATA *work on oblivious to the* THREE TAUNTERS.)

FIRST TAUNTER: Look at them wildly searching for a magic bullet.

SECOND TAUNTER: They've done that two hundred . . .

THIRD TAUNTER: Year in . . .

FIRST TAUNTER: Three hundred . . .

THIRD TAUNTER: Year out . . .

SECOND TAUNTER: Four hundred . . .

THIRD TAUNTER: Always failing . . .

FIRST TAUNTER: Five hundred . . .

THIRD TAUNTER: Never successful. . . .

SECOND TAUNTER: Six hundred times they have done it. Paul Ehrlich is a mad fool!

THIRD TAUNTER: A failure.

FIRST TAUNTER: Why don't you give up, Paul Ehrlich, you and that little Japanese S. Hata? (*The lights dim from the* THREE TAUNTERS *and grow more intense on* EHRLICH *and* HATA.)

EHRLICH: . . . the principle of this is right. We know that. We twist and turn these arsenic compounds first one way and then another. We must find a magic bullet to kill the disease.

HATA: Are these formulas to be tried next?

EHRLICH: Try them. Try them. Always keep trying.

HATA: Yes, sir.

EHRLICH: Arsenic will kill a human being. But if we find the right combination of arsenic we will kill the spirochete in the patient and not the patient himself.

HATA: This tube? How much?

EHRLICH: Add three cc.'s of chloride! That may be the one we're looking for. (*The light emphasizes the* THREE TAUNTERS *again.*)

FIRST TAUNTER: He tries again!

SECOND TAUNTER: He will fail again.

THIRD TAUNTER: This is the 606th time. I've counted.

FIRST TAUNTER: Six hundred and six times a fool.

SECOND TAUNTER: A mad fool!

(*Light emphasis shifts back to* EHRLICH *and* HATA.)

HATA: Meister! Look!

EHRLICH: What is it?

HATA: This is the 606th compound we have the report on.
It was used on five rabbits last week. All had ugly sores.

EHRLICH: Yes. . . .

HATA: All are alive and the sores are gone!

EHRLICH: I knew it. The magic bullet. It is the salvation
of man. It will cure! It will save. I give the world my
salvarsan!

FIRST TAUNTER: What!

SECOND TAUNTER: He has found the cure.

THIRD TAUNTER: Bravo for Paul Ehrlich.

FIRST TAUNTER: Such courage!

SECOND TAUNTER: He never gave up!

THIRD TAUNTER: A genius!

FIRST TAUNTER: We knew Paul Ehrlich could do it!

Blackout

SCENE THREE

CHARACTERS

A VOICE	FIRST LEGISLATOR
FIRST GIRL	SECOND LEGISLATOR
SECOND GIRL	SPEAKER
FIRST WOMAN	THIRD LEGISLATOR
SECOND WOMAN	FOURTH LEGISLATOR
THIRD WOMAN	FIFTH LEGISLATOR
FOURTH WOMAN	

A VOICE: The year of our Lord, 1933!
(*Three spotted areas are picked up successively in front of the curtain.*)

FIRST WOMAN: Ja, it wouldn't be so bad, but some of them are respectable educated people. First it was 606, then it was fever treatments and now it's bismuth. Why in the world don't they put their intelligence to something worth while, I say. Why, I understand they even print those silly articles in the medical journals. Ja, that's the place for them, all right.

Blackout

(*Light up in second area.*)

FIRST GIRL: Did you hear that up in Wisconsin a man can't get married unless he takes a medical examination first?

SECOND GIRL: Ain't that awful. They're not asking the girls to do that, too, are they?

FIRST GIRL: Oh, heavens, no. They'd never dare ask a girl to do that. What do they think we are?

Blackout

(*Light up in third area.*)

FOURTH WOMAN: What made me mad was, he asked for blood for a Kahn blood test. And I was gonna do it, too, till I learned it was a new test for syphilis.

THIRD WOMAN: I would have walked right out of his office.

FOURTH WOMAN: That's exactly what I did. I was never so insulted in my life.

Blackout

(*Light up in first area.*)

SECOND WOMAN: . . . and that's what we're payin' taxes for . . . to keep guys like that in office. Why, just the other day someone was tellin' me that a guy named Saltiel was going to discuss syphilis right on the floor of the state legislature. Imagine that! My God, what's the world comin' to?

Blackout

(*The lights rise on the Lower House of a State Legislature. The* FIRST LEGISLATOR *is speaking.*)

FIRST LEGISLATOR: . . . the proposition is to add an amendment to the law in relation to marriage. This modern amendment to an old law would require persons of both sexes to present a medical certificate stating they are free from venereal diseases. In submitting this amendment I wish to call attention to the great damage done by syphilis and gonorrhea each year. Statistics show that syphilis and gonorrhea . . .

SECOND LEGISLATOR: Mr. Speaker, I object to the terms being employed in this discussion.

FIRST LEGISLATOR: To what terms do you refer?

SECOND LEGISLATOR: It should be quite obvious to what terms I refer.

FIRST LEGISLATOR: Unless you can be more specific I shall continue the speech begun. I see nothing objectionable in it.

SECOND LEGISLATOR: Well, I do. I may be old-fashioned and come from a small town but I still believe that the dignity of the legislature should not be besmirched by anything so patently revolting. The diseases to which references have been made are incompatible with anything above the level of bar-room talk. Furthermore, most of us are fathers of children who would sooner or later be subject to this infamous law. How many of us would wish them to be humiliated by an examination before the most sacred, the most holy moment of their lives? This amendment presupposes suspicion of a most intolerable nature. In the name of decency I demand that this discussion be dropped at once!

FIRST LEGISLATOR: Mr. Speaker, with all due respect to my sensitive colleague, I insist that the greatest menace confronting public health today is syphilis. Each year its deadly effect on the social structure becomes more apparent. . . .

SPEAKER: Pardon me, but are you really serious in what you're saying or is this some sort of joke?

FIRST LEGISLATOR: I've never been more serious in my life!

THIRD LEGISLATOR: Mr. Speaker, I refuse to remain on the floor while this disgraceful discussion continues!

FIRST LEGISLATOR: If the gentleman was only aware of the significance of this measure.

FOURTH LEGISLATOR: Possibly the answer is that you'd like a civil service job examining prospective brides! (*The others laugh at this.*)

FIRST LEGISLATOR: I refuse to be swayed by my colleague's vulgar stupidity.

FIFTH LEGISLATOR: May I seriously ask what your interest in this amendment is?

FIRST LEGISLATOR: To that I gladly reply. Up until a year ago I had no interest in it whatever. It was one of those vague subjects one hears but never discusses. Then I was made a member of an investigating committee for the insanity board. I visited a few of our insane hospitals. There I saw the wrecked, ravaged flesh of madmen perishing from this disease. Huddled in corners I saw their wasted bodies, many of them crying to be dead. And I thought it would be a kind God that would give them death in place of their miserable sufferings. But I knew society is not as merciful as that. But if we can't release these people through death we can at least stop breeding them. And that, gentlemen, is the purpose of this amendment! (*There is an embarrassed pause.*)

SECOND LEGISLATOR: I'm sure that my colleague, being a young man, is being a bit too melodramatic in this matter. We would be alarmed, too, if we did not know that this disease confines itself to those of loose morals and criminal instincts—the riff-raff of society. I insist it has no place in a bill dealing with anything as honorable and sacred as marriage.

FIRST LEGISLATOR: Mr. Speaker, I ask that this be put to a vote.

THIRD LEGISLATOR: Sit down, Ed, we're all blushing for you.

FOURTH LEGISLATOR: My constituents would kick me out of office if they knew I came to discuss bills like this.

FIRST LEGISLATOR: Mr. Speaker, there's an amendment before the floor. I demand that it be voted upon.

SPEAKER: In order to save Sir Galahad from further embarrassing the House we shall proceed to the next bill.

FIRST LEGISLATOR: I demand a vote.

SPEAKER: You're out of order! The gentleman from Drool County has the floor.

FIFTH LEGISLATOR: Mr. Speaker, I present the bill for enlarging our program for eradicating noxious weeds. Each year the farmers of this state are losing money because of pigweed, burdock, thistle, ragweed. . . . The effect on hay fever is devastating. These weeds must be stamped out! (*There is thunderous applause at this as the lights* . . .)

Blackout

SCENE FOUR

CHARACTERS

A VOICE	JOHN ELSON
MR. THOMAS	THE WIFE
MISS JOSLYN	TONY

THE DOCTOR	FIRST LEGISLATOR
POLITICIAN	SPEAKER
SECOND CLERK	SECOND LEGISLATOR
FIFTH LEGISLATOR	THIRD LEGISLATOR

A VOICE: The year of our Lord, 1936!

(*The executive offices of a large industrial plant. At the rise of the lights* MR. THOMAS *is seated at his desk.* MISS JOSLYN, *his secretary, is finishing the work of the day. It's about five in the afternoon and the slanting rays of the sun fall across the desk, fading toward the end of the scene.*)

THOMAS: That'll be all for this afternoon, Miss Joslyn. See you in the morning.

MISS JOSLYN: Aren't you going to see him?

THOMAS: See who?

MISS JOSLYN: That man from the shop who's been waiting outside your door all afternoon.

THOMAS: Good heavens, is he still here?

MISS JOSLYN: Yes, he is, sir, and he looks rather pathetic. He must be one of the men you laid off.

THOMAS: If he's been laid off there must be a reason. I don't want to see him.

MISS JOSLYN: I've already told him you would.

THOMAS: Oh, well, show him in. Might as well get it over with.

MISS JOSLYN: Yes, sir. (*She goes to the door and admits* JOHN *to the office.* JOHN *is a man of thirty-six who looks older than his years. He is a very frightened man right now*) Mr. Thomas will see you now.

JOHN: Thank you.

MISS JOSLYN: Will that be all, Mr. Thomas?

THOMAS: Yes, I guess so. Good night, Miss Joslyn.

MISS JOSLYN: Good night. (MISS JOSLYN *goes.* JOHN *stands timidly near the door.*)

THOMAS: I didn't get your name. . . .

JOHN: John Elson, sir.

THOMAS: John Elson? Oh, yes, yes, I remember. Well, what's on your mind, John?

JOHN: This, sir. I don't quite understand. (*He places a blue slip before* THOMAS.)

THOMAS: Your discharge, eh? Didn't Mr. Morrison speak to you?

JOHN: Yes, he did, but I still don't understand. I don't know what I've done to get this, sir. I've been employed here a long time. Ten years. I've never been late. I never cause trouble.

THOMAS: It isn't a question of being late or causing trouble, John. We appreciate faithfulness. Wish we had more men like you. But the insurance company through Mr. Morrison seem to think you're a risk they can't very well carry.

JOHN: I've always done my best. I try hard.

THOMAS: It isn't a question of trying, John. We know you like the work and we hate to lose a willing workman. But from the code on this slip it seems you're not as careful as you once were, that you get into little accidents which they believe avoidable. The insurance company will overlook one accident—like cutting your finger there —but when it happens three times they begin to wonder.

JOHN: But I've worked here a long time. Nothing serious has ever happened.

THOMAS: No, they step in before anything serious does happen. It all comes under the head of general inefficiency.

JOHN: But I've worked here a long time. This is only the second job I've had in my life. I don't know where I'd go.

THOMAS: How old are you?

JOHN: Thirty-six, sir.

THOMAS: Thirty-six? I thought you were older than that.

JOHN: No, that's my right age. I wouldn't lie.

THOMAS: There's no reason why you should be fired for a thing like this at thirty-six. You should be at the peak of your ability at that age.

JOHN: It's the only kind of work I know.

THOMAS: I can't understand it. Occasionally we have to lay off men when they reach fifty, cruel as it seems, because the system is too complicated for them. They become a danger to others as well as themselves. But you're not old, John, and yet we're firing you because you seem old.

JOHN: Of course I'm not old.

THOMAS: Maybe you worry too much. Mr. Morrison said your mind strayed from your work. What's been bothering you, John?

JOHN: Nothing, unless . . .

THOMAS: Unless what, John?

JOHN: Unless it's because my wife's going to have a baby.

THOMAS: Why should that worry you? Do you have any other children?

JOHN: Only one living. We lost two when they were babies. Oh, we've had our share of hard luck. But we never complained. Only this—losing my job—that's something we never counted on.

THOMAS: You make me feel very badly, John. I wish I could help you.

JOHN: You could give me back my job.

THOMAS: No, much as I'd like to, I can't do that. We've got a schedule to maintain and can't break it up for one man. Furthermore the insurance company won't carry you on their accident compensation list.

JOHN: You mean I'm definitely fired?

THOMAS: Yes, John, I'm afraid you're definitely fired!

Blackout

SCENE FOUR—A

(In the darkness the voice of JOHN'S *wife is heard. She is reading from a book.)*

THE WIFE: ". . . with that he swept the scythe through the grass, full of ox-eye daisies, and sighing with a dry sound. And because the grass was so thin, you could watch the scythe, like a flash of steely light, through the standing crop before the swath fell. And it seems to me now it was like the deathly will of God, which is ever waiting behind us till the hour comes to mow us down; yet not in unkindness, but because it is best for us that we leave growing in the meadow, and be brought into His safe rickyard, and thatched over warm with His everlasting loving-kindness."

(The lights, which have risen during this, reveal the wife reading to a blind boy of twelve. He listens attentively until she is done.)

TONY: Are there any pictures with it, Ma?

THE WIFE: Not in this book, dear.

TONY: I wish there were.

THE WIFE: What difference does it make, Tony?

TONY: I like to think of pictures. I'd like to make some of my own. Big ones with all the colors you could think of, green, orange, pink, and what are the other colors?

WIFE: Blue, red, yellow, brown, lavender—ah, there are many colors, Tony.

TONY: Read on.

THE WIFE: That was the end of the chapter.

TONY: Start a new chapter.

THE WIFE: It's too late for that.

TONY: Pa isn't home from work yet. It can't be late.

THE WIFE: Yes, it is, Tony. He's late. I can't understand

what's keeping him. (*She has put the book down and begins to pace the room nervously.*)

TONY: Why are you worried?

THE WIFE: I'm not worried. I'd like to know where he is, that's all. He's not been well lately. He won't admit it but I can tell.

TONY: You always tell me not to worry. You say I shouldn't worry about not seeing again.

THE WIFE: I know, Tony, it's foolish of me. Tony, I think you better go to bed. You're tired.

TONY: You always say, "Tony, you're tired," and you don't really know if I'm tired at all. Do you?

THE WIFE: Tony, please go to bed.

TONY: Just as you say. (*He gets up and starts to go*) Well, all I can say is, there's one good thing about not being able to see.

THE WIFE: What's that?

TONY: You're not afraid of the dark. (*He stops half way across the room*) Wait a minute. There's Pa now.

THE WIFE: How do you know?

TONY: Why doesn't he come in? He's out there.

THE WIFE: Are you fooling me, Tony?

TONY: Open the door and see. (*She opens the door and there is* JOHN. *He looks more frightened than ever, his face is pale.*)

THE WIFE: John! Why are you standing there?

JOHN: Why, I was . . .

TONY: See, I told you. I knew he was there.

(JOHN *comes in looking very bedraggled. The* WIFE *starts to say something but* JOHN *puts up a finger and warns her not to show her fear before* TONY.)

JOHN: How are you tonight, Tony?

TONY: I'm fine, Pa. Ma just read me a good story but it didn't have pictures. Why are you late?

JOHN: I was kept at work.

TONY: Did they pay you extra, Pa?

JOHN: No, this was something else. I thought you'd be in bed by now.

TONY: I was on my way when you came. And I think I'm going to miss something now but I'll go anyhow.

THE WIFE: Good night, Tony. Don't kick the covers off you. It's cold in your room.

TONY: You better tie my feet down then. (*And* TONY, *familiar with the room, makes his way out without help. As soon as he is gone the* WIFE *rushes to* JOHN *who has slumped in a chair.*)

THE WIFE: John, what happened?

JOHN: Everything, Martha, everything.

THE WIFE: But tell me.

JOHN: I will tell you. But I've got to get my wits first.

THE WIFE: You frighten me.

JOHN: I'm frightened myself. I don't know where to begin.

THE WIFE: Yes . . .

JOHN: Well, I might as well get it all out at once. Martha, you can't have the baby!

THE WIFE: I can't have the baby! But it's three months . . . A little late to change my mind . . . it's . . .

JOHN: It doesn't matter, you can't have it.

THE WIFE: John, you're trembling. Don't tremble. Why can't I, what do you mean?

JOHN: I was fired today.

THE WIFE: No!

JOHN: Yes! They've let me go. Said I was too old for the work. Said I was like an old man.

THE WIFE: They couldn't have meant it. You've been so faithful there.

JOHN: I've been faithful all right. Oh, God, Martha, it was crazy the way they talked. But they let me go just the same, and you mustn't have the baby.

SPIROCHETE

83

THE WIFE: You're taking it too hard. You'll find another job.

JOHN: You don't know why I was fired, the real reason.

THE WIFE: Why were you fired?

JOHN: I didn't know at first. They didn't know either. They just said I couldn't keep up with the schedule. And that's true, Martha. Lately the work's been too hard. The same work I used to do without any effort at all began getting too hard for me. So when they let me go I was afraid to come home and tell you.

THE WIFE: John, you should never be afraid of me.

JOHN: Well, I was. I was afraid of myself. I walked the streets for a long time. Then I went to our doctor and asked if there was any medicine he could give me. I thought he could give me something so I wouldn't be so tired.

THE WIFE: Did he?

JOHN: He examined me. He examined me all over, my nerves, my blood, everything.

THE WIFE: What did he say?

JOHN: Martha, I found out why Tony's blind!

THE WIFE: You—you found out why Tony's blind? Why?

JOHN: Because of us.

THE WIFE: Why because of us? Aren't we all right?

JOHN: The doctor said no. He said I've been sick for a long time, and most likely you've been sick, too.

THE WIFE: What kind of sickness?

JOHN: The doctor said it's—it's syphilis. (*She stifles a scream while* JOHN *continues*) I didn't know I had it. I still don't know how I got it. I used to see those stories in the papers but I never dreamed it was me—me who might have it. He said it doesn't pain you at all. . . . It just comes quietly.

THE WIFE: It must have happened long ago.

JOHN: It must have. Long before I met you.

THE WIFE: Oh, God, John, what'll we do?

JOHN: He said we shouldn't be frightened. He said we shouldn't worry.

THE WIFE: At least now we know. Now there's no question. We know why you lost the job.

JOHN: And we know about Tony.

THE WIFE: Yes.

JOHN: Martha, the doctor said you should come to him, too.

THE WIFE: So we won't have the baby.

JOHN: I don't know.

THE WIFE: Yes, I understand. We couldn't have another. Like Tony, he'd never have a chance.

JOHN: None of us had a chance, Martha, none of us had a chance! (*He falls weeping on her lap.*)

Blackout

SCENE FOUR—B

(*The scene is* MR. THOMAS's *office again. At the rise of the lights, the* DOCTOR *is talking to* MR. THOMAS.)

THE DOCTOR: . . . and so a few months ago this John Elson came to my office asking for medical examination. He said he'd been fired from your company for inefficiency and he wondered if there was anything I could do for him.

THOMAS: Yes, I remember the case. We hated to let him go. He had always been a willing worker.

THE DOCTOR: I wonder if you realize the real reason for his inefficiency?

THOMAS: We try to look into those things when we can but of course it's impossible to investigate all personal details.

THE DOCTOR: How often do you have to dismiss a man for inefficiency—for getting into accidents, for making mistakes, for star-gazing, for day-dreaming, for wasting time?

THOMAS: It happens quite frequently. We're a large organization.

THE DOCTOR: And breaking in a new man is a rather expensive item, isn't it?

THOMAS: Yes, terribly. But we have to accept it as part of our industrial system—this hiring and firing of men.

THE DOCTOR: Would you like to know why one man—this John Elson, for instance, who worked here for more than ten years—was lost to you?

THOMAS: It wasn't our fault, I can tell you that. His pay was good, his working conditions ideal.

THE DOCTOR: Well, I'll tell you why. The reason he was inefficient was because he had syphilis.

THOMAS: I don't believe it. He's not the type.

THE DOCTOR: The disease doesn't confine itself to types, Mr. Thomas. It's liable to strike anybody. John, in a rather unusual case, had gotten it innocently years ago. Because of ignorance of the symptoms he never even knew he had it.

THOMAS: He must have.

THE DOCTOR: No, he didn't.

THOMAS: Well, I'm glad he's gone. We don't want any such man around this plant.

THE DOCTOR: He wouldn't have had the disease if you had helped him.

THOMAS: How could I have helped him?

THE DOCTOR: You could have given all your men blood tests at regular intervals. You do all other things to avoid inefficiency.

THOMAS: That's too personal a problem.

THE DOCTOR: It will save you money, you know.

THOMAS: What's that?

THE DOCTOR: I said it would save you money.

THOMAS: How do you explain that?

THE DOCTOR: Oh, don't think I'd expect you to do all this out of sheer good-heartedness. Far from it.

THOMAS: But saving money. How will I go about that?

THE DOCTOR: Take blood tests of all your men. Find out how much potential inefficiency you've got in your plant.

THOMAS: That's an excellent idea. Then we could lay off all the men who look like bad risks.

THE DOCTOR: Oh, no, not so fast here. You can't do that. You won't get any man tested until you can assure him that the test will in no way interfere with his job—provided he takes treatment. If they're under treatment they'll be as efficient as anybody.

THOMAS: You're sure of that?

THE DOCTOR: I wouldn't be here if I didn't think so.

THOMAS: All right. I'll take it up with the board of directors at once. And I can promise you this—if, as you say, it will increase the efficiency of our men, which means more money for us, I know the board will adopt it.

THE DOCTOR: All right, now that we have that settled, what about John?

THOMAS: John? Well, he's already fired and the disease has got the best of him. We couldn't take him back, could we?

THE DOCTOR: He'll end up on the relief rolls if you don't. And you'll pay for that in the long run anyway.

THOMAS: But he'll be a danger to the other men.

THE DOCTOR: Do you think so? I wish you'd look at him. (*The* DOCTOR *goes to the door*) John, will you come in here a minute. (JOHN *enters looking very strong and healthy. The* DOCTOR *turns to* MR. THOMAS) He'll be no more of a menace than you or I.

THOMAS: Why, John, you don't look like the same man. How do you feel?

JOHN: Never better. I feel ten years younger and I'm ready to start work—that is, if you'll take me.

THE DOCTOR: I think you'd be making a mistake if you didn't, Mr. Thomas.

THOMAS: Well, doctor, if you're sure the cure is permanent, I don't see any reason why he can't have this job back.

JOHN: Thank you, Mr. Thomas. I'm sure you won't regret it.

THOMAS: But there's one thing I'm a bit curious about. Maybe I seem a bit sentimental, but what about the baby you said your wife was going to have. Won't that be rather dangerous?

THE DOCTOR: Even the unborn are not beyond our reach. The baby will be all right. We can begin treatments as late as the fifth month and in ten cases out of eleven the child will be normal. The main thing is to test by the Kahn or the Wassermann and find out where this disease is lurking. If John had been tested at the time of first employment he would have known this. If he had been tested at the time of marriage it could have been prevented. Industry must do its part. The people and the State must do theirs. . . .

Blackout

SCENE FIVE

(*The music rises for a moment and the lights rise before the curtain outside the floor of a Legislature.*)

VOICE: The year of our Lord, 1937!

(*The* POLITICIAN *and the* SECOND CLERK *are discovered before the curtain.*)

POLITICIAN: Okay, maybe a law like that's all right. But the question is: what's it gonna do to us? Every lousy couple will leave the state to get married. They won't wait for no examination. And where's that gonna put our little Gretna Green here, huh?

2—2

THE SECOND CLERK: Oh, no, it don't. Not if I can help it. It's up to you and me to see it don't get passed, see. (*The* FIFTH LEGISLATOR *enters. The* POLITICIAN *looks up pleasantly surprised*) Oh, oh, look who's comin'. (*He goes up and buttonholes the* FIFTH LEGISLATOR) Well, well, well, if it ain't the gentleman from Drool County. Imagine that. Have a cigar, fella. Boy, you can't imagine how glad I am to see you. Say, that's a good-lookin' suit ya got on. Where'd you get it? It sure looks good on you. It's all right. (*They go off stage together and the* THIRD *and* FOURTH LEGISLATORS *enter. The* SECOND CLERK *goes up to them.*)

THE CLERK: Good morning, gentlemen. Lovely morning, isn't it? Wish we'd have more mornings like this, don't you? It makes a person feel peppy, doesn't it? Here, have a cigar. (*They accept and look at each other questioningly*) Nothing so good for a person as feeling peppy, is there? It sort of makes you feel like voting the right way, doesn't it? (*The* POLITICIAN *returns.*)

POLITICIAN: Gentlemen! Imagine meeting you here. (*He goes up to embrace them*) Here, have a cigar. My gosh, it's sure a small world after all.

Blackout

(*The curtain rises on the floor of the Legislature. The* FIRST LEGISLATOR *is speaking.*)

FIRST LEGISLATOR: Mr. Speaker, four years ago I presented a bill which, over my protests, was not recognized by the chair.

SPEAKER: If the gentleman from Cook County is again referring to an amendment to the marriage code, I might advise him that the feeling of this House has not changed.

SECOND LEGISLATOR: But the feeling of the people has changed. Look! (*He points to the side and rear where many people have gathered*. They demand that this amendment be heard!

SPEAKER: If my memory serves me correctly it was your opposition to the bill four years ago that led to its suppression.

SECOND LEGISLATOR: I admit it. I admit my own former blindness to facts which ought to have been obvious to all of us. But since that time I have learned that a country like Sweden wiped out this disease because years ago it faced the facts and didn't try to hide them. Based on past records we know that out of one hundred thousand Americans this year, 796 will be struck down by syphilis. Out of exactly the same number of Swedes, only seven will get it. Seven hundred and ninety-six to seven is the difference between blindness to facts and intelligence applied to those same facts.

THIRD LEGISLATOR: But this isn't Sweden. What works there might not work here.

FIRST LEGISLATOR (*jumping up to join the debate*): All right. Let me tell you the story of Denmark then. Last year in America sixty thousand babies were born with syphilis. Sixty thousand helpless children had this disease wished on them through no fault of their own. But while we were breeding sixty thousand sickly babies—not counting the other thousands who died before birth—while this was going on, Denmark gave birth to five.

SECOND LEGISLATOR: And I say that even if this isn't Sweden, even if this isn't Denmark, the things they can do, we too can do! (*There is a commotion at the side as the* POLITICIAN *tries to push his way through.*)

POLITICIAN: Gangway here. Let me through here.

SPEAKER: Order! Order! (*He bangs his gavel to quiet the crowd.*)

SECOND LEGISLATOR: During the past four years I have learned many things. My eyes have been opened to the flagrant weakness of any system that allows its people to suffer year after year. Let's be truthful with ourselves.

POLITICIAN *(shouting)*: The bill can't be passed. (*The people shout at him to be quiet. The* SPEAKER *cries for attention.*)

SECOND LEGISLATOR: I say, let's be truthful with ourselves. Nice people do get syphilis. And I say the difference between those who do and those who don't is misfortune and nothing else. The syphilis carrier is a potential murderer and must be stopped whether he likes it or not!

POLITICIAN: No!

THE PEOPLE: Yes!

FIRST LEGISLATOR: Let this be put to a vote.

SPEAKER: All those in favor signify by saying aye! (*Everyone shouts aye in a great chorus which is taken up by the people. The* SPEAKER *bangs for attention and his request for "nay" votes is drowned out.*)

SPEAKER: The amendment stands adopted! (*There is applause for this*) Victory for this amendment is a battle just begun. Votes for a measure mean nothing unless translated into action by the people. This fight must go on until syphilis has been banished from the face of the earth. It can be done and will be done if you and you and you wish it so. The time has come to stop whispering about it and begin talking about it . . . and talking out loud!

The curtain falls